TEACHING STRUGGLING READERS WITH POETRY

Engaging Poems With Mini-Lessons That Target &
Teach Phonics, Sight Words, Fluency & More—
Laying the Foundation for Reading Success

Maria P. Walther & Carol J. Fuhler

SCHOLASTIC

New York • Toronto • London • Auckland • Sydney
Mexico City • New Delhi • Hong Kong • Buenos Aires

DEDICATION:

To Lenny, you add poetry and laughter to my life. Happy twentieth anniversary!
— M. P. W.

With love to Dick, who continually supports my efforts to be a writer, and a heartfelt thanks to my sister-in-law, Eunice Fuhler, who welcomed Dick and me into her home as temporary guests and let me adopt her screened porch and inspiring lake views as I worked to complete this book.
— C. J. F.

Editor: Gloria Pipkin
Cover design: Brian LaRossa
Interior design: LDL Designs
Cover photo: Maria Walther
Interior photos: page 22 © Corbis; all others: Maria Walther and Lauren Leon
Copy editor: Carol Ghiglieri

ISBN-13: 978-0-545-15682-0
ISBN-10: 0-545-15682-3
Copyright © 2010 by Maria P. Walther and Carol J. Fuhler
All rights reserved. Published by Scholastic Inc.
Printed in the U.S.A.

1 2 3 4 5 6 7 8 9 10   40   16 15 14 13 12 11 10

CONTENTS

ACKNOWLEDGMENTS

We are grateful to . . .

Carole Boston Weatherford, Bobbi Katz, and Marian Reiner, on behalf of Eve Merriam, Myra Cohn Livingston, and Aileen Fisher, who generously adjusted their permission fees to make our dream of putting inspiring words into the hands of readers a reality. An additional thanks to Jill S. Goodman at Boyds Mills Press, who facilitated the adjusted rates for the poems by Brod Bagert, Jane Yolen, Rebecca Kai Dotlich, and Eileen Spinelli.

Gloria Pipkin, who is unmatched as an editor and an inspiration as a friend. You march through whatever life throws your way and still make time for us. You and Miss T. help us create books with the pizzazz and perfect punctuation that our readers deserve.

Virginia Dooley: This book is a result of your belief that we could take a small idea from *Literature Is Back!* and create an entire book. Thanks for inviting us back!

Becky and Pete Anderson and all of the knowledgeable book enthusiasts who work at Anderson's Bookshop in Naperville, Illinois—you are our partners as we work diligently to put exceptional books in the hands of teachers and children.

The following publishers: Abrams, Boyds Mills Press, Candlewick, Disney Hyperion, HarperCollins, Houghton Mifflin, Lerner, and Macmillan, who help us stay on top of the latest and greatest books.

Katherine Phillips, friend and colleague. You've been there through thick and thin and are always willing to think with me when I need one more comprehension lesson, another idea for teaching vocabulary, or a piggy-back song about fossils! (Maria)

POETRY ACKNOWLEDGMENTS

"A Book" by Myra Cohn Livingston. From MY HEAD IS RED AND OTHER RIDDLE RHYMES by Myra Cohn Livingston. Copyright © 1990 by Myra Cohn Livingston. Used by permission of Marian Reiner.

"A Cabin" by Katie Walther. From IMPRESSIONS OF YOUTH. Copyright © 2004 by Katie Walther. Reprinted by permission of The American Library of Poetry.

"Cat Kisses" by Bobbi Katz. "Cat Kisses" Copyright © 1974 by Bobbi Katz and renewed 1996. "When I'm An Astronaut" Copyright © 1990 by Bobbi Katz. Used with permission of Bobbi Katz, who controls all rights.

"Caterpillars" by Aileen Fisher. From CRICKET IN A THICKET by Aileen Fisher. Copyright © 1963 by Aileen Fisher. Copyright renewed © 1991 by Aileen Fisher. Used by permission of Marian Reiner on behalf of the Boulder Public Library Foundation, Inc.

"A Circle of Sun" by Rebecca Kai Dotlich. From LEMONADE SUN AND OTHER SUMMER POEMS by Rebecca Kai Dotlich (Wordsong, an imprint of Boyds Mills Press, 1998.) Reprinted with the permission of Boyds Mills Press, Inc. Text copyright © 1998 by Rebecca Kai Dotlich.

CHAPTERS 2-5 LESSON GUIDE

Chapter 2: Welcome! Poems About School, Friendship, and Family	Chapter 3: Adventure! Animal Poems	Chapter 4: Perform! Playing With Poems	Chapter 5: Imagine! Poems to Take You Away
"The Eraser" * • Teaching Idea • Phonics: *Hard C, Soft C* • Writing	**"Guess"** * • Comprehension: Inferring • Meaning Vocabulary: *"Three Read-Aloud Words"* • Meaning Vocabulary for ELLs	**"Shout"** * • Fluency • Meaning Vocabulary: Word Banks • Writing	**"I Know a Way to Open Doors"** • Teaching Idea • Phonics: Making Words—*Treasure* • Fluency
"Crayons: A Rainbow Poem" * • Comprehension: Inferring • Sight Vocabulary • Meaning Vocabulary for ELLs	**"The Shark"** • Phonemic Awareness: Syllables • Comprehension: Comparing Texts About the Same Topic • Meaning Vocabulary: Synonyms	**"Jump or Jiggle"** • Phonemic Awareness: Rhyming Versus Non-Rhyming Words • Meaning Vocabulary: Action Verbs • Writing	**"When I'm an Astronaut"** * • Sight Vocabulary • Meaning Vocabulary: Compound Words • Writing
"Friendship" • Phonemic Awareness: Rhyming Words • Phonics: Differentiating Between Rimes and Rhymes • Fluency	**"Whale"** • Fluency • Comprehension: Thinking About Characters • Sight Vocabulary: Family Word Bingo	**"Chant of the Awakening Bulldozers"** • Fluency • Meaning Vocabulary • Writing	**"Rickety Train Ride"** • Phonics: *Consonant Blends—/cl/ and /tr/* • Fluency • Writing
"When Hannah Moved Away" • Phonics: Consonant Blends • Fluency • Writing	**"A Rumba of Rattlesnakes"** * • Phonemic Awareness: Alliteration • Fluency • Meaning Vocabulary: Verbs	**"A Circle of Sun"** * • Phonics: *Word Endings—(-ing)* • Meaning Vocabulary: Antonyms • Writing	**"Junior Geographer"** * • Fluency • Meaning Vocabulary: Geography Words • Meaning Vocabulary for ELLs
"A Family Is . . ." * • Comprehension: Building Background Knowledge • Writing	**"The Lizard"** • Phonics: Word Families—(-ing) • Meaning Vocabulary: An Alphabet of Action Verbs	**"Whooo?"** • Phonemic Awareness: Medial Sounds • Phonics: *Digraphs—/wh/* • Fluency	**"A Book"** * • Phonics: Word Families—(-ay) • Comprehension: Elements of a Mystery • Meaning Vocabulary: Antonyms
" Brother" • Phonemic Awareness: *Beginning Consonant—/b/* • Phonics: *Word Endings—(-er)* • Fluency	**"The Coyote"** • Phonics: *Word Sort—/owl/ vs. /own/* • Writing	**"Me X 2"** • Meaning Vocabulary: Homophones • Fluency • Comprehension: Thinking About Characters	**"Cat Kisses"** * • Phonics: *Digraphs—/ch/* • Comprehension: Mental Images
"My Sister Is a Sissy" • Phonics: *"is" Contractions* • Meaning Vocabulary: Synonyms	**"I Would Like to Have a Pet"** * • Phonics: Word Families—(-all) • Comprehension: Activating Schema • Writing	**"City Music"** • Phonics: Making Words • Fluency	**"The Toaster"** • Fluency • Meaning Vocabulary: Homophones • Writing
	"The Monster's Pet" • Phonemic Awareness: Playing With Nonsense Words • Phonics: Word Families—(-et) • Sight Vocabulary	**"Manhattan Lullaby"** • Phonemic Awareness: Syllables • Phonics: Word Families—(-eep) • Comprehension: Conversing and Connecting	
	"Wishes" • Meaning Vocabulary: Compound Words • Writing		

* Denotes reproducible poem

CHAPTERS 6-8 LESSON GUIDE

Chapter 6: Investigate! Poems to Enhance Science Instruction	Chapter 7: Experience! Poems for the Seasons	Chapter 8: Write! Poems That Inspire Writers
"Caterpillars" * • Phonemic Awareness: Beginning Blend Substitution • Phonics: *Word Sort—/ow/ vs. /ew/* • Comprehension: Nonfiction Text Structures—Question and Answer	**"Groundhog"** * • Phonics: *Word Sort—/ee/ vs. /ea/* • Comprehension: Predicting • Meaning Vocabulary: Word Concept Chart	**"Pencils"** * • Teaching Idea • Meaning Vocabulary: Quiet Words and Noisy Words • Writing
"Caterpillar" • Phonemic Awareness: Syllables • Fluency • Writing	**"Galoshes"** • Phonics: *Blends—/sl/ and /st/* • Fluency • Writing	**"The Magic Wand"** • Comprehension: Conversing and Connecting • Sight Vocabulary • Writing
"I Like Bugs" • Fluency • Writing	**"March Wind"** • Fluency • Comprehension: Point of View • Meaning Vocabulary: Action Verbs	**"Quiddling With Words"** * • Phonics: *Consonant Blends—/br/, /cr/, /gr/* • Comprehension: Visualizing • Meaning Vocabulary: Dictionary Usage
"Heads or Tails" * • Phonics: *Word Endings—(-ed)* • Comprehension: Point of View • Meaning Vocabulary: Action Verbs	**"A Cabin"** * • Fluency • Comprehension: Author's Purpose • Writing	**"Treasure Words"** • Teaching Idea • Phonemic Awareness: *Initial Consonant—/s/* • Writing
"Dirty Socks" • Phonemic Awareness: Listening for Rhymes • Phonics: Making Words—*Pollution* • Fluency	**"Playing Outfield"** • Phonics: Word Families—(-op) • Meaning Vocabulary • Writing	**"Clatter"** * • Phonics: Word Families—(-ack) and (-ock) • Fluency • Writing
"A Worm" • Phonemic Awareness: *Initial Consonant—/w/* • Meaning Vocabulary: Prefixes • Meaning Vocabulary for ELLs	**"Baseball Surprise"** • Fluency • Phonics: Long Vowels—Silent e • Meaning Vocabulary	**"Whirr, Whirr, Zing, Zap"** • Fluency • Meaning Vocabulary for ELLs • Writing
"Polliwogs" • Phonics: *Short Vowels—/u/* • Fluency • Writing	**"Snow"** * • Phonics: The Different Sounds of /ow/ • Fluency • Meaning Vocabulary: Compound Words	
"The Pond's Chorus" • Fluency • Sight Vocabulary: Number Word Bingo • Writing	**"We'll Play in the Snow"** • Phonics: Differentiating Between Rimes and Rhymes • Meaning Vocabulary: Categorizing • Writing	
"Fossils Here, Fossils There" * • Fluency • Comprehension: Building Background Knowledge	**"Silence"** • Phonemic Awareness: *Initial, Medial, and Final Sound—/t/* • Fluency • Comprehension: Compare and Contrast	
"Dinosaur Bone" • Comprehension: Questioning • Sight Vocabulary	**"Fall Is Here"** • Phonemic Awareness: Listening for Rhymes • Comprehension: Extending Meaning • Writing	
"Sleeping Beside a Stegosaurus on an Overnight Class Trip to the Museum" • Sight Vocabulary • Meaning Vocabulary: Antonyms • Writing	**"Labor Day"** • Phonics: *Diphthong—/oi/* • Sight Vocabulary • Meaning Vocabulary for ELLs	

WHO NEEDS POETRY?

by Carole Boston Weatherford

Who needs poetry?
Kids who like rhythm,
Kids who like rhyme,
Kids on the fast track,
Kids who take their time,
Kids who keep journals,
Kids who love to write,
Kids who curl up with a book
on warm and cozy nights.

Who needs poetry?
Kids who watch too much TV
and think reading's a bore,
Kids who hate writing
and find that math's a chore,
Kids who are laid back,
Kids who won't sit still,
Kids who are motor-mouths,
Kids who want to chill.

Who needs poetry?
Kids who like to sing,
Kids who feel the beat,
Kids who like motion,
Kids with dancing feet,
Kids who like word play,
Kids who like to rap,
Kids who crave a little treat
to savor in a snap!

Source: *Everyday Poetry* (Vardell, 2009)

THE PROMISE OF POETRY

We are enthusiastic and excited about the promise of poetry for all young readers, and we especially endorse its possibilities for children struggling to read. We want to pay our excitement forward, hoping that you will catch it and pass it on to your students. For those battling to make sense of the printed word, a short, silly, repetitive poem might offer a glimmer of success. Reassuring as a steady heartbeat, the rhythm of a poem could focus another child helping her memorize it, bouncing a bit to the underlying beat. Before long, the familiar words will be recognized in other texts, too. When you read poems to and with your students, laughing at those that are outrageous or puzzling out an intriguing new word together, you will be building a warm and accepting learning environment. That's a reassuring place to be when you're having difficulty learning to read, isn't it?

Is poetry magic? Well, maybe a little. It becomes more so when you love it. Share it with a twinkle in your eye. Interpret it with your voice, reading quietly when describing snowflakes and raising the volume when introducing demanding bulldozers. Draw from it to teach a quick, essential reading strategy. Turn to it for an impetus for writing. Let it help children build fluency as they read, read, read it together and alone. We believe that poetry can't be beat for sharing the joys hidden within the printed word.

As you delve into the upcoming chapters, you will find a cross-section of fabulous poetry to share with your students. Many poems are reproducible so that you and the children will have them at your fingertips. We found others with great teaching possibilities, and for these we give you the sources where you can locate them and accompanying mini-lessons. We paired poems with related picture books, offering more opportunities for reading and discussion, so the learning goes on. Slipped between some chapters are slices of key research accompanied by additional teaching ideas. We hope these materials will whet your appetite, sending you to colleagues, the librarian, and your favorite bookstores to augment this sampling. In the meantime, welcome to *Teaching Struggling Readers With Poetry*. We couldn't be more pleased that you're here!

CHAPTER 1

USING POETRY TO TEACH STRUGGLING READERS

> **"Verse Play" by Eve Merriam**
> The poem's a ball
> cupped in your hand,
> open your fingers
> and let it drop—
>
> wait,
>
> stop,
>
> bounce it back
> and catch the rhyme
> just in time
> in time, in time.
>
> Source: *The Singing Green* (Merriam, 1992)

Poetry: Serve It Up Daily

Poetry. It can be outrageous or somber, nonsense or a serious reflection on life. It is written about mundane things like pencils and safety pins or vast things like fathomless oceans and the endless universe. It might pinpoint the delicacy of a snowflake or marvel at the bulk of the hippopotamus. It comes in shapes, rhymes, free verse, haiku, and more. It blossoms when read aloud, but soothes when savored in solitude. Poetry is many things to many people. Some people are drawn to it; others back away, a little unsure. Poetry will enrich your lessons and become an enjoyable change of pace for you and your students. It has a bounty to offer. Serve it up daily, especially to those who are struggling to master reading. We're here to tell you why. But first . . . .

You are holding this book in your hands because, like us, you're continually searching for effective, research-proven ways to boost the reading skills of your young learners. Perhaps you have a handful of students (or maybe the majority of your class) who are struggling to learn to read. Some children may be lacking rich background experiences in literacy, while others are learning a second language. Still others simply can't seem to unlock the letter-sound code. Sadly, for many of them, motivation may be waning as they attempt to keep pace with their peers. Whatever the case may be, you need practical, research-based strategies to teach them in joyful and motivating ways. Rest assured—you've come to the right place. We can think of no better way to engage even the most reluctant reader than with an enticing poem.

Pause for a minute and think of these possibilities. You might reach for anthologies like *The Random House Book of Poetry for Children* for a myriad of poems on child-appealing topics selected by former Children's Poet Laureate Jack Prelutsky (1983). Then, mix in a selection of books that focus on one topic, such as *Sports! Sports! Sports!* by Lee Bennett Hopkins (1999) or Douglas Florian's *Comets, Stars, the Moon, and Mars* (2007). Round these out with poems written by children in your classroom. Armed with a motivating collection of poems, from anthologies to rhythmic storybooks, you're sure to catch the interest and build the necessary skills for learners whose ability to read remains elusive.

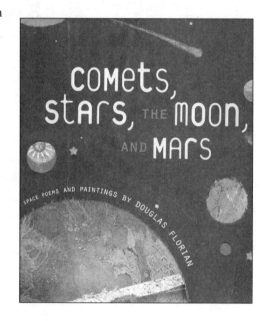

In this book, you will find poetry-based mini-lessons designed to help readers with the essential aspects of literacy. Each lesson will model how you can use the reproducible focus poem to teach key reading skills, including phonemic awareness, phonics, fluency, vocabulary, and comprehension, as well as writing, which we view as an essential component of effective reading instruction. The focus poem is followed by additional poetry suggestions and mini-lesson ideas to reinforce and extend the learning with poems that are easily located in your school or local library. To further supplement the mini-lessons found in each chapter, we've included five inserts entitled *Reading Research + Poetry: Ready-to-Use Ideas* that contain additional research-proven teaching ideas. We've created this book as a jumping-off point to get you and your learners started on a road to success. You are the best person to identify the lessons that will meet your students' specific learning needs and to select the poems that will kindle their interest. We hope that these lessons, coupled with your creativity, will strengthen literacy skills while adding smiles to the faces of your young readers.

Before we start on the lessons, let's take a moment to look to the experts in the field and then identify what our research-guided experience tells us struggling readers need.

What Do Struggling Readers Need? Research-Guided Principles

Why do some students struggle, while others seem to learn to read so effortlessly? The answer to this question is as individual as each child you greet at your classroom door. Thus, our interactions with children are paramount. Every learner benefits from thoughtful, responsive literacy instruction. Whether a child is a proficient reader or a beginner, his needs are the same. When you apply the following principles to your teaching, all students will benefit from motivating and focused instruction.

Stimulate students' interest and you create readers!

KNOWLEDGEABLE TEACHERS

First and foremost, struggling readers need YOU! Study after study (Allington, 2002; National Education Association Task Force on Reading, 2000; Reutzel & Cooter, 2008) shows that teachers are the most important factor in improving students' reading achievement. Literacy expert Richard Allington states that "Effective teachers manage to produce better achievement regardless of which curriculum materials, pedagogical approach, or reading programs they use" (2002, p. 742). Literacy researcher Jane Braunger and literacy professor Jan Lewis (2006) underscore this premise when they write that it is excellent teachers and not published programs that create independent, thoughtful, and engaged readers. You know these researchers are right. So do we. Here are some important points for you to consider as you fine-tune your reading instruction.

First, young students need an enthusiastic role model when it comes to reading and writing. That's you. Second, in terms of content, they need material that is worth teaching and learning, which you select with an eye to curriculum standards and tailor to each student. Third, to keep anxiety at bay, they need a classroom home that is a welcoming, comfortable, and accepting learning environment (Hadaway, Vardell, & Young, 2001). Then, because these learners are not sure of themselves, they will profit from your immediate, descriptive feedback on their efforts. Not only is this motivating, but it also boosts their meager levels of confidence. Descriptive feedback includes more than saying the oft-repeated but vague "Good job!" Specific feedback helps readers build a sense of agency and independence (Johnston, 2004). For example, when a reader makes a miscue, you might say something like:

"Something didn't make sense, did it? What can you do?"

"As a reader, what should you do?"

When students decode a word, say, "You figured out that tricky word by yourself. How did you figure that out?"

Next, children blossom when they have choices. Perhaps you let them select among books, poems, activities, or writing opportunities, when appropriate. Having that element of choice is motivating in and of itself (Pressley, Dolezal, Raphael, Mohan, Bogner & Roehrig, 2003; Rasinski & Padak, 2004). Most important, you are there to cheer your learners on and to celebrate their successes, large and small. You believe that they can and will succeed.

Create an inviting classroom environment brimming with books.

In addition, take the time to get to know your learners, ask them about their interests, and find out what matters most to them—what makes them tick. Bolster that information with formal and informal assessments to uncover their reading strengths and difficulties. Naturally, the more you know about your students, the easier it will be to scaffold instruction to meet their needs. Think about setting different goals for individual students (Tomlinson, 1999; Wood, 2002). This is a year-long effort as you monitor student growth and adjust materials and expectations accordingly, always with student success uppermost in your mind.

> **Struggling Readers Need . . .**
>
> Enthusiastic role models
>
> Engaging learning materials
>
> Inviting classroom environments
>
> Immediate, descriptive feedback
>
> Frequent opportunities for choice within structure
>
> Focused instruction tailored to their interests and learning needs

MOTIVATING INSTRUCTION

One key to designing motivating instruction builds on your knowledge of each student (Brophy & Good, 1986). In the rush to teach everything that is expected, we sometimes forget that we are teaching readers, not a reading program. We are guiding readers, not teaching guided reading lessons. The first step in motivating our students is to use what we know about them to carefully select materials and learning opportunities that capitalize on their background knowledge and curiosities (Gambrell, 2001). For instance, if you have a child like Austin, who loves to go fishing, locate reading materials about fishing and encourage him to write his own list of supplies (right) needed to catch a fish.

How do you create a motivating classroom environment? If you walked into Maria's energy-filled

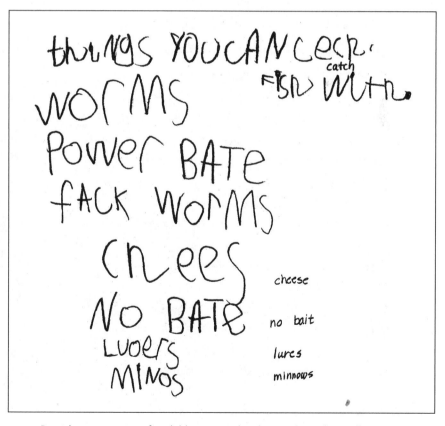

Provide opportunities for children to read and write about things they enjoy.

first-grade classroom, you would see motivated children in action. In addition to the preceding ideas, here are others that Maria believes work with her young learners:

- Create consistent, daily routines for literacy instruction and independent practice.
- Engage in conversations with students about what they notice and what they are thinking.
- Celebrate students' thinking, even if it is different from your own.
- Establish clear expectations; explain *why* the skills they are learning are important.
- Teach explicitly, and then provide support and scaffolding as students try something on their own.
- Encourage students to rethink and revise their thinking as they add new learning.
- View mistakes as learning opportunities.
- Value the process more than the product.
- Provide opportunities for varied-size group instruction.
- Model, model, model.

Additional Suggestions for Motivating English Language Learners

- Use materials about familiar subjects, building on background knowledge and interests.
- Select authentic and meaningful texts.
- Choose books and poems in which the language is clear and concise.
- Be certain the vocabulary is age-appropriate.
- Limit text that contains idioms and figurative language unless these can be easily explained.
- Read aloud stories and poems that contain repetitive language to build vocabulary and fluency.
- Select materials with accompanying illustrations that can help children better understand the text.
- Work in pairs and triads, encouraging cooperative learning.
- Celebrate special days and well-known people that are a part of the children's cultures.
- Gather books in each child's native language, so that they can build skills in that language, too.

(Fuhler & Walther, 2007; Graves, Juel, & Graves, 2007; Reutzel & Cooter, 2008)

Use this colorful book to kick off a Day of the Child celebration.

POWERFUL READING INSTRUCTION

What do we mean by powerful reading instruction? With the increased pressure to ensure that all of our learners are making adequate progress, we must search for the most effective instructional components for our core reading instruction. When we strengthen our instructional practices, all students benefit, and those who need extra support and intense instruction make greater gains.

Frequent Read-Aloud Experiences

One of the reasons many of us decided to become primary-grade teachers is that we love books and enjoy sharing them with children. Whether you are a classroom teacher, reading specialist, literacy coach, or invaluable support teacher, we're sure you have a collection of your favorite books at your fingertips ready to help your students learn to and love to read. Some of them might be poems or stories with rhythm and rhyme. Poetry just begs to be read aloud, doesn't it?

Researchers have shown that the benefits of reading aloud are plentiful (Allen, 2003; Anderson, Hiebert, Scott, & Wilkinson, 1985; Trelease, 2006). Among them is the fact that reading aloud develops children's interest in books and fosters a positive attitude toward reading. Frequent read-aloud experiences are vital for struggling and reluctant readers because listening to rich literature selections enables readers of all abilities to enjoy a story, nonfiction book, or poem. As an added bonus, reading aloud "enhances reading motivation, develops genre knowledge, and even develops core curricular knowledge" (Allington, 2005, p. 224). To that end, you might read a selection of Valerie Worth's *Animal Poems* (2007) or *Butterfly Eyes and Other Secrets of the Meadow* (Sidman, 2006) to partner with your science unit.

Components of Powerful Reading Instruction

Frequent read-aloud experiences

Engaging conversations

Playful phonemic awareness activities

Explicit phonics instruction

Robust vocabulary teaching

Meaningful fluency development activities

Thoughtful comprehension lessons

Multilevel, flexible small-group instruction

Ample time to read independently

Effective writing instruction

Integrated content area studies

ANIMAL POEMS

Valerie Worth *Pictures by* Steve Jenkins

Benefits of Reading Aloud

- Develops a sense of story

- Builds students' background knowledge

- Introduces new vocabulary in rich contexts

- Models what good reading sounds like

- Demonstrates reading for a purpose

- Enables children to hear interesting sentence patterns

- Teaches about various styles of writing

- Provides models and ideas for student writing

- Motivates children to read more, including rereading the story the teacher just read

- Creates a community of readers through enjoyment and shared knowledge

(Anderson et al., 1985; Fountas & Pinnell, 1996; Hadaway et al., 2001)

To add to your read-aloud fare, we've included suggestions of picture book pairings to accompany the poems. These pairings offer your students an opportunity to read about a particular topic across different genres, broadening not only their content knowledge but also their awareness of different types of literature. Along with the poems and picture book pairings, each chapter includes a chart entitled "Poetic Picture Books and Themed Anthologies" to enrich and extend the learning in pleasurable ways. Without a doubt, adding poetry to your core reading curriculum is an additional motivator that we firmly believe you will all enjoy.

Engaging Conversations

You might find that some of your struggling readers shine in the discussion arena. Each year in Maria's first-grade classroom, she has a student or two who, although they have dif-

For additional suggestions for using quality children's literature to teach reading and writing, see *Literature Is Back!*

ficulty with the act of reading, engage in thoughtful discussions about the books and poems that she reads aloud. This daily talk time is essential for all students, but it is especially important for our English language learners and struggling readers because conversation facilitates understanding. We don't all take away the same things from what we read. Talking together enables children to exchange ideas and to consider others' opinions and interpretations of the text (Dunston, 2002; Rasinski & Padak, 2001). This sharing of knowledge, whether in the whole group, mixed-ability groups, or in pairs, also helps these learners build background knowledge in order to better understand present and future text (Pearson & Fielding, 1996; Pressley, 2002). Ardith Cole (2003) highlights other reasons for conversations when she comments that talking together teaches children

> *…to crawl between the lines and dredge out the inferences and innuendos, [and to see] how they take a stand and support it with textual evidence, and how they make connections to their own lives, other texts, and the craft of the author. (p. xiv)*

When we spend less time on worksheets and more time on focused dialogue, we find that talk time is a powerful tool for all of the learners in our classroom.

To frame these conversations, we rely on the wise thoughts of researcher Peter Johnston in his book *Choice Words* (2004):

- *Encourage students to notice things in the literate world such as rhyming words, a poet's use of creative conventions, or the way a poet chose to arrange the words on a page.*

- *Address all students simply as readers and writers. Try the words, "That's just what readers do!"*

- *Refrain from using the term "good" readers as that implies that there are also "bad" readers.*

Playful Phonemic Awareness Activities

Phonemic awareness is the knowledge that spoken language comprises small units of sound called phonemes and the ability to manipulate these sounds. Children who are phonemically aware are able to notice,

Talking together allows readers to exchange ideas and to consider others' opinions and interpretations of the text.

mentally grab hold of, and manipulate phonemes—the smallest chunks of speech (Yopp & Yopp, 2000). Phonemic awareness is an area of difficulty for many struggling readers. Luckily, many of the activities that target phonemic awareness are rooted in language play, poetry, and song. The phonemic awareness activities you will find tied to upcoming poems will be playful, focused on the sound structure of spoken language, and easily woven into your comprehensive reading instruction.

Explicit Phonics Instruction

As we noted earlier, a lack of letter-sound knowledge impedes students' progress as readers. In most schools a systematic phonics program is already part of the core reading instruction. Why does systematic phonics work for struggling readers? It works because the brain is a pattern detector. Therefore, word-based activities that help readers use the patterns of our language to decode unknown words are key to successful phonics instruction. Incorporating research-proven, engaging activities such as the formation of words, high-frequency word recognition using the word wall, and the study of word families (Cunningham, 2009a) will boost your phonics instruction. In fact, "for many at-risk readers, systematic phonics instruction is probably close to a cure for their beginning reading problems, at least at the word recognition level" (Pressley, Gaskins, & Fingeret, 2006, p. 52). When we pair engaging, systematic phonics instruction with poetry, it is a win-win scenario for all.

Robust Vocabulary Teaching

Think about how many words you say and read in just one day in your classroom. It's difficult to come up with a number, isn't it? Just to play with numbers a bit, ponder this. An average 6-year-old could enter the classroom with a vocabulary that ranges from 2,500 to 5,000 words, depending on background experiences, books read aloud at home, a second language spoken at home, or other variables. That's quite a range. By the time the average child completes eighth grade, she might know about 25,000 words. That number could swell to 50,000 at high school graduation (Graves, 2006). Of course, it doesn't stop there because we continue to expand our vocabulary throughout our lives.

To acquire some of those words, wide reading is strongly endorsed by researchers in the field. Unfortunately, reading widely is a challenge for our struggling readers. As a result, you will have to rely more on read-alouds to build vocabulary, selecting titles on a variety of topics from a collection of memorable books (Allen, 2003; Rasinski & Padak, 2004). To be certain students actually learn new words, plan on a good deal of focused, direct teaching of selected words. Then, practice, practice, practice.

The majority of researchers believe that school-age children become aware of seven new words a day, but they still have to work with them to actually learn them (Beck & McKeown, 1996). For students trying to master reading, that number will be reduced to two or three. Remember that to really know a word, children have to use it and use it again, up to as many as 40 times, before it becomes their own. Thus, repeated encounters with new words through reading, talking, and writing will cement an understanding of those words over time (National Reading Panel, 2000).

Meaningful Fluency Development Activities

In reviewing a number of definitions of fluency, we found that the consensus seems to be that fluency refers to accurately and effortlessly reading connected text at a conversational rate using the right phrasing and expression, while drawing the intended meaning from that text (Hudson, Lane, & Pullen, 2005; Ming & Dukes, 2008; Rasinski, 2006). Fluency experts Tim Rasinski and Nancy Padak remind us, "Fluency is the bridge between word recognition and comprehension" (2001, p. 172). So, it *is* important.

Fluent readers can focus on the meaning of what they are reading because for them decoding is automatic and effortless. Children who do not read fluently are at a disadvantage because their comprehension suffers. For them, reading is a labor-intensive process as they sound out one word at a time. So much of their consciousness is involved with processing each word that there is little left over for understanding (Pressley et al., 2006). We offer several sound methods for helping students improve word recognition through poetry that will undeniably improve their fluency.

Whatever methods you use to help your struggling readers build fluency, it is best to teach each method directly. Less skilled readers need intentional instruction along with sufficient time spent in fluency-focused practice to improve this skill. Research has shown that fluency can be developed in a number of ways. Try different methods with your learners depending on their assessed needs (Pressley et al., 2006). In this book, we will focus on three practices: modeling fluent reading through read-alouds, supporting students in a choral reading format, and having students engage in repeated oral reading (Faver, 2008; Rasinski, 2003, 2006).

Thoughtful Comprehension Lessons

Our goal for all readers is that they are able to think deeply about what they've read and to share this thinking with others. Thoughtful comprehension lessons encourage students to read and think at the same time—to go beyond the written word and connect with the author's message. Powerful reading instruction emphasizes comprehension. Using poetry as a vehicle, we've designed mini-lessons to help you teach students how to flexibly use the strategies that proficient readers employ—such as making connections, asking questions, inferring, visualizing, and determining important ideas during and after their reading. Keep in mind as you sample the comprehension mini-lessons in this book that each one is easily adapted to meet the needs of your readers or to match other texts that are part of your reading instruction.

Multilevel, Flexible Small-Group Instruction

It makes sense that to meet the needs of the diverse learners in your classroom, you will need to create opportunities to work with students in different grouping arrangements. While this book does not describe in depth how to organize and manage small group interactions, it does provide a wealth of lessons that are ideal for working with an individual or a small group of students (National Reading Panel, 2000; Pressley et al., 2006; Reutzel & Cooter, 2008). Cole (2003) remarks that, based upon her classroom experience, triads can be a most effective group size, making it easy to sit "knee to knee and eye to eye." A bonus for smaller groups is that in twos, threes, or fours, even the quietest or least confident voice can be heard.

A caution is to avoid ability grouping, which places lower-achieving students at a distinct disadvantage. In this arrangement, they suffer from knowing they are in the lowest group. Such placement douses their self-esteem and motivation, which can promote a negative attitude toward reading (Allington, 2006; Fountas & Pinnell, 1996). Instead, strive for flexible, heterogeneous groups that vary from project to project.

Work with students in a small group to guide them as they practice reading skills and strategies.

This decision will enable children to work with everyone in the classroom throughout the year, increasing their opportunities and motivation to learn (Graves et al., 2007; Reutzel & Cooter, 2008).

Ample Time to Read Independently

The more students read, the better readers they become (Allington, 2002; Garan & DeVoogd, 2008; Pressley, 2000). When we offer students daily opportunities to read texts that are "just right" for them, we boost all of their reading skills. This is especially important for struggling readers (Ming & Dukes, 2008). While reading, learners have the opportunity to consolidate their skills and strategies, eventually making them a natural part of their reading behavior (Allington, 2002). Then, with stronger skills, they are more inclined to read. You have begun a cycle of success that revolves around your focused teaching of new skills, which then leads to more successful reading (Pressley, 2002), and to practice that continually strengthens all skills. But, what should they be reading?

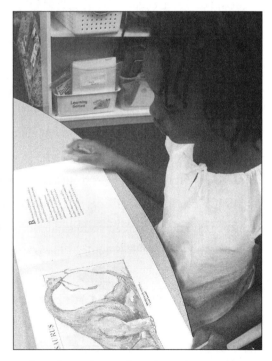

Provide ample time for independent reading.

Many of us try diligently to find books that are the perfect fit for our struggling readers. Fortunately, the world of poetry offers a tempting array of choices for even the most finicky reader. Students who love to laugh can't get enough of Jack Prelutsky's silly poems, while animal lovers enjoy Douglas Florian's books, such as *Dinothesaurus* (2009) or *Lizards, Frogs, and Polliwogs* (2001). Once you get students hooked on poetry, you'll find they want more and more (Fuhler & Walther, 2007). We've collected as many poems and related resources as we could pack into one book. We also offer suggestions for additional poems for students to seek out on their own. Enjoy sleuthing with your students to find just the right anthology, picture book, or Web source to provide plentiful reading.

Effective Writing Instruction

In addition to providing our struggling students with ample time to read books, we recognize that they also benefit from time to write. For beginning readers, writing develops their phonemic awareness and phonics knowledge as they encode (stretch out, chop up, or sound out words) while writing. The act of encoding requires a much higher level application of phonics knowledge than identifying letters and sounds in isolation, and it increases their ability to decode words in their reading. In addition to strengthening phonics knowledge, writing develops students' sense of story. As young writers learn how to compose stories, nonfiction pieces, and poems, they firm up their understanding of the same text structures in their reading.

Integrated Content Area Studies

With instructional time at a premium, you might be in a situation where you are being encouraged to forgo your science and social studies instruction to make more time for literacy lessons. Wise teachers like you know that a more sensible way to do this is to integrate your content areas topics into your reading and

Writing and reading go hand in hand.

writing lessons. When children experience integrated content area instruction, they are increasing the size of their meaning vocabularies and their general knowledge base while discovering real reasons to read and write (Cunningham & Allington, 2007). Using poetry to kick off a unit or asking students to write a poem to summarize their understanding of a topic not only fosters interest but also boosts literacy skills.

Why Use Poetry to Teach Struggling Readers?

In identifying the key components of core reading instruction that support our struggling readers, we've suggested the areas of focus for your instruction. Now, we set out to show you how poetry is a perfect fit for reaching the most reluctant readers. Why are we so enthusiastic about using poetry with struggling readers? Over and over we've seen that reading poetry helps build confidence and fluency in all children (Fuhler & Walther, 2007; Hadaway et al., 2001). You will quickly see how mastery of a short poem through lots of repetition and rhyme can build students' self-confidence (Sekeres & Gregg, 2007; Wilfong, 2008). Another reason is that poetry is perfect for choral reading (Yopp & Yopp, 2003). This style of reading lets the voices of hesitant readers blend with those that are more confident, protecting self-esteem. With additional practice, even those faltering voices will ring with confidence. Then, too, poetry enables you to teach word recognition strategies and to build vocabulary skills within its brief text. Building that base of stronger word knowledge in turn increases comprehension (Wilfong, 2008). Not to be overlooked is the fact that poems touch our emotions, perhaps promoting a little more self-understanding or understanding of others in the process. One might argue that the best reason of all is that poetry makes us smile when we sample its nonsense, word play, and humor (Galda & Cullinan, 2006). Below we offer a few more compelling reasons to use poetry. No doubt you can add to this powerful list of reasons to teach through poetry based upon your own experiences.

IT'S SHORT!

For struggling readers, poetry is ideal. They look at the brevity of poems, surrounded by lots of white space, and sigh with relief. Short poems are so much less intimidating than many stories found in basal anthologies or trade books. To help students who needed reading interventions, Lori Wilfong (2008) created a Poetry Academy when she was working as a literacy coach in an elementary school. She opted for poetry because of the short text: It was easy fare for repeated readings, and it was fun. While she made a point of searching for poems that were humorous, children in general also favor poems about family life and animals, and those that tell a brief story (Fuhler & Walther, 2007). The results of Lori's work were heartening because readers improved and reported enjoying the process. Your learners will, too.

IT PLAYS WITH LANGUAGE

Poems provide an ideal occasion to play with language. This oral language play is the foundation for developing and enhancing your students' phonemic awareness. Well-chosen poems set the stage for fast-paced

Winners of the NCTE Award for Excellence in Poetry for Children

Lee Bennett Hopkins (2009)	Lilian Moore (1985)
Nikki Grimes (2006)	John Ciardi (1982)
Mary Ann Hoberman (2003)	Eve Merriam (1981)
X. J. Kennedy (2000)	Myra Cohn Livingston (1980)
Eloise Greenfield (1997)	Karla Kuskin (1979)
Barbara Juster Esbensen (1994)	Aileen Fisher (1978)
Valerie Worth (1991)	David McCord (1977)
Arnold Adoff (1988)	

phonemic awareness activities. For example, children can listen for and identify rhyming words or repeat the alliterative phrases to isolate beginning sounds.

When you're looking for poems that feature particularly effective ways to play with language, consult the award-winning poets above. Honored by the National Council of Teachers of English for their exceptional contributions, these could become poetry partners over the coming year. To assist you in finding their poems, we've included the work of these talented poets throughout the book either on a reproducible poetry page or as a suggested poem for follow-up teaching.

IT COMPRISES WELL-CHOSEN WORDS

Sometimes grin-inducing, and other times simply a pleasure to read, the words in poems are carefully chosen. They may tickle the tongue and revolve around and around in your brain long after you've read or recited them. Poetry offers an authentic context for students to apply their developing phonics knowledge. You can build on the time and effort that poets have spent as they searched for exactly the right words to tell a bit of a story or to create an image. You might do so by identifying irresistible noisy words that illustrate onomatopoeia. Discuss these and other exceptional words or rhythmic phrases and have the children repeat them with you. Understanding how carefully their poetry partners use words will benefit your students as they read and appreciate other poems and when they write their own.

IT INCORPORATES RHYTHM AND RHYME

The rhythm, rhyme, and repetition of a poem serve as scaffolds for deciphering its meaning. In addition, the rhythmic language of poetry lends itself to choral reading, repeated oral reading, and Readers Theater, all research-based fluency-boosting practices. See for yourself what happens when you read poetic picture books with rhythm and rhyme. For instance, your dinosaur lovers are sure to join in when they hear the opening lines of *Saturday Night at the Dinosaur Stomp* (Shields, 1997). To continue this excitement, you will find a wealth of fluency-building options in the pages to come.

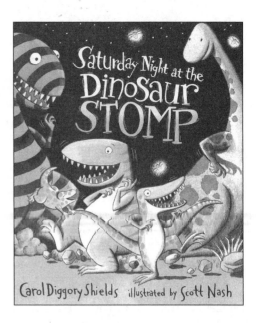

IT CONTAINS RICH VOCABULARY

Poetry is just the ticket to provide word practice. Whether you are discovering the meaning of new vocabulary words or targeting words for young readers to recognize by sight, poems are ideal for highlighting and creating interest in words. In her book *What Really Matters in Vocabulary*: *Research-Based Practices Across the Curriculum* (2009b), renowned literacy expert Patricia Cunningham shares a sensible vocabulary-building strategy that she calls "Three Read-Aloud Words." Cunningham suggests targeting three words from one read-aloud selection each week. She dubs read-aloud words "Goldilocks" words—words that are not "too easy" (generally known by most of your students) or "too hard" because they're uncommon or obscure. Once you've selected the target words, follow the lesson sequence she's created:

1. Read the text for pleasure.
2. Show the target words to your students on index cards, one at a time. Teach your students to pronounce each word, but ask them not to share the meanings so that you can demonstrate the strategies that readers use to acquire new word meaning during reading. Place the words where your students can see them.
3. Reread the text and invite your listeners to yell "STOP!" when they hear a target word. At this point, stop reading and demonstrate for your readers how you use the context, illustrations, and word parts to figure out and explain the meaning of that particular word. Continue with the two other words.
4. After reading, ask questions to help readers connect the words to their own experience.
5. The next day, reread the text and ask students to retell the text to a partner using the target vocabulary words.
6. Display the words in your classroom next to the cover of the book or poem. Then, challenge students to be on the lookout for these words. Place a tally mark next to each word that a student

reads, hears, or notices in print. Your challenge is to also try to use these words in your conversations throughout the week.

Several examples of poetry books that could foster vocabulary building are *A Crossing of Zebras: Animal Packs in Poetry* (Maddox, 2008); *A Whiff of Pine, A Hint of Skunk* (Ruddell, 2009); and *Bees, Snails, & Peacock Tails* (Franco, 2008).

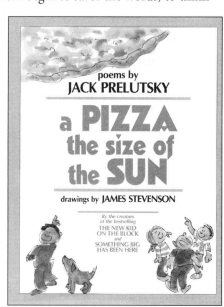

IT BOOSTS COMPREHENSION

Poets paint pictures with words. Their use of sensory language helps children see, hear, taste, and touch the images their words create. Struggling readers are often spending so much time focusing on decoding the words they don't pause to visualize the author's message. We can use poetry to help them begin to savor the words, to think and read at the same time. For example, when we read aloud the poem "My Elephant Is Different" by Jack Prelutsky, found in *A Pizza the Size of the Sun* (1996), children draw their own version of the elephant whose "ears are short and fuzzy" and add to the picture "its tail [that] is like a mushroom on its tiny blue behind." Although poems provide endless opportunities to visualize the author's message, they are also helpful when teaching many other comprehension strategies, as you will discover in the mini-lessons that follow. Certainly, well-chosen poems will assist you as you teach students all of the comprehension strategies that proficient readers naturally employ as they read.

IT CREATES INTEREST IN A TOPIC

For children who are not confident in their reading abilities, content area texts can be overwhelming (Cunningham & Allington, 2007; Fuhler & Walther, 2007). The vocabulary is a challenge, as is the layout of many books. As you deftly teach them to master this content, use poetry as one of your tools. For example, when the experts tell us, "There must be a concerted effort to foster academically and intellectually rigorous learning of subject matter [for English language learners] while they are developing their English-language abilities" (Valencia & Buly, 2004, pp. 529–530), we can meet such demands with a brief but engaging poem (Hadaway et al., 2001). To ease into content area topics or an upcoming nonfiction story on the changing seasons, you might try reading selections from NCTE award-winning poet Barbara Juster Esbensen's book *Swing Around the Sun* (2003). When you open the doors to learning in such an inviting way, you not only raise curiosity but you will also have an opportunity to begin discussions that will build background knowledge, too.

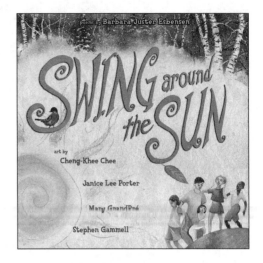

IT SPARKS ENTHUSIASM FOR WRITING

Students who find reading a challenge often don't see themselves as writers. When you weave poetry into your literacy lessons, young learners benefit from being surrounded by the words of seasoned writers. They see and hear how poets use figurative language, creative conventions, rhythm, rhyme, and much more to express their thoughts and ideas. In fact, "children are more likely to become poets if they have plenty of time to sample, savor, and discover the joys of well-written poems" (Walther & Phillips, 2009, p. 127). Literacy consultant Lori Oczkus and her colleagues Gery Baura, Kathy Murray, and Karen Berry (2006) found benefits to immersing students in fine poems, teaching them how to write poetry, and then encouraging young writers to try it with support. The benefits of writing poetry they identified include the following:

- Enhances narrative writing
- Creates successful writing opportunities for struggling and reluctant writers
- Frees ELLs to experiment with language without worries about syntax and conventions
- Challenges proficient writers to apply their creativity as they share their ideas in a unique way

Certainly, when you mix poetry into your literacy instruction, you will spark enthusiasm for the written word and create another avenue for struggling students to find success.

IN THE END . . .

As readers enter our classroom
They trust that we will help them bloom
With books and words, concern and care
We gather them close and begin to share
Poems that wiggle, giggle, and shout
Poems that make them grin or pout
Poems read in whispers
Poems sung out loud
Poems will certainly please the crowd
With poetry, they can reach their goals
As we fill their ears and hearts and souls.

CHAPTER 2

WELCOME!
POEMS ABOUT SCHOOL, FRIENDSHIP, AND FAMILY

Celebrate Poetry

Who needs poetry? You and your students do! To create joyful learning opportunities, celebrate language, and boost the reading skills of even the most reluctant reader, make poetry a part of your classroom routine. Welcome your learners on the first day of school—and each day that follows—with a smile and a collection of enticing poems. We've selected the first few poems in this chapter to use as you create a classroom community that supports all readers, especially those who are struggling. In addition, you'll find poems about school, family, and the ups and downs of friendship.

Along with using poems to teach essential literacy skills, consider adding a Poetry Break to your busy schedule. It will change the rhythm when planned lessons bog down or spark energy for learning across the curriculum. You'll soon be looking for reasons to slip in a poem here and there throughout the day. When working with the poems in this book, it will be helpful if you enlarge a copy for all to see. You may do this by writing the poem on sentence strips and placing it in a pocket chart or by using an overhead projector or document camera. In addition, provide individual copies for students to keep in a special poetry binder. The poetic options for reading and rereading will help build fluency in the upcoming months as children choose poems to read with a partner, take the binder home to read with the family, or pick a favorite poem to read aloud during a Poetry Break.

Another way to entice readers to pick up a poem is by having a designated space in your classroom to house poetry books. Clear off a section of a shelf or place poetry books in a colorful basket. To keep interest high, rotate books periodically. When you have an extra moment or two, read a book from the basket. When reading poetry anthologies, kindergarten teacher Paula Loret de Mola invites her students to pick a number; she then reads the poem or poems that appear on that particular page. To guide students as they begin to discover their poetry preferences, ask them to review the poem by assigning it a 1- to 4-star rating, along with their reasons for liking or disliking the poem. Along with reading poems aloud, encourage students to select a poem to rehearse during independent reading or at literacy centers. One child may perfect a choice to read aloud by herself. Several children could present a favorite chorally. Another student can lead the class in echo-reading his poem. In addition, a Readers Theater performance could be just right for a longer poem or a rhythmic picture book. Encourage children to experiment with various methods as they gain more confidence in reading. Once students are ready to perform, invite them to write their names on a strip of paper and place it in the "Poetry Performance Jar." When you have a few minutes during a transition time or at the end of the day, draw a name from the jar and watch poetry come to life.

Poetry Pointer: "Who Needs Poetry?"

Get your students moving with Carole Boston Weatherford's poem found on page 8. Read it together several times. Clap out the beat or snap fingers to the rhythm. Then try it "popcorn" style, where one designated child at a time pops up to read a line (Vardell, 2009). As you read and reread together, you'll be illustrating the irresistible role of rhythm and rhyme as well as modeling a perfect practice for building fluency.

Poems That Celebrate Books, Poems, and Reading

POEM	FOUND IN . . .
"Booktime" by Avis Harley (p. 27)	*Falling Down the Page* (Heard, 2009)
"The First Book" by Rita Dove (p. 1)	*Poetry Speaks to Children* (Paschen, 2005)
"Good Books, Good Times!" by Lee Bennett Hopkins (p. 17)	*Good Books, Good Times!* (Hopkins, 1990)
"I Am the Book" by Tom Robert Shields (p. 18)	*Wonderful Words* (Hopkins, 2004)
"The Library" by Barbara A. Huff (p. 220)	*The Random House Book of Poetry for Children* (Prelutsky, 1983)
"The Library Cheer" by Brod Bagert (Unpaged)	*Shout! Little Poems That Roar* (Bagert, 2007)
"Look! Look!" by Jack Prelutsky (p. 99)	*My Dog May Be a Genius* (Prelutsky, 2008)
"Two Lives Are Yours" by Richard Armour (p. 98)	*Days to Celebrate: A Full Year of Poetry, People, Holidays, History, Fascinating Facts, and More* (Hopkins, 2005)

Mini-Lessons for "The Eraser" by Brod Bagert

TEACHING IDEA

Use this poem as a catalyst for a whole-group conversation about treating others in the classroom with courtesy and respect. As part of the discussion, talk about the need to think before acting so that no one will have to try to "erase" a hurtful comment or deed. After your discussion, work

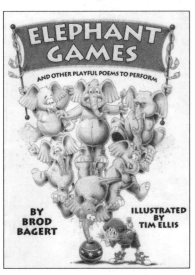

Poetry Pointer: Poems That Celebrate Books, Poems, and Reading

From week one onward, you can demonstrate your love of reading and the role it plays in your classroom through poems we've located that celebrate the written word. See the chart, Poems That Celebrate Books, Poems, and Reading, above. Emphasize the rhythm in these poems by reading each through once. If the poem is a little tricky in parts, model the rhythm during a second reading, verse by verse. Have students echo-read each verse after you. Once you have worked through the poem, reread it chorally at a pleasing pace and invite students to quietly clap the rhythm. To improve fluency, pick up the speed as you enjoy this poem over the next few days.

THE ERASER
by Brod Bagert

I made a lot of mistakes today.
Twelve minus five does not equal eight.
Carrot does not start with K.
And *"No, stupid, you cannot sit next to me!"*
Was not a nice thing to say.

I erased the eight and wrote seven.
I erased the K and wrote C.
But nothing can erase the tears
You cried because of me.

So I wrote this little poem
To find a way to say,
I'm sorry.
Please forgive me
For hurting you today.

Source: *Elephant Games and Other Playful Poems to Perform* (Bagert, 1995)

with your students to compose a chart of "Respectful Behaviors" or a "Classroom Promise" (Miller, 2002) similar to the one that appears at right to help make your classroom a safe and caring place to learn. Once the list is complete, ask each child to reread it and sign their name at the bottom, then post for all to see.

PHONICS: HARD C, SOFT C

Write the word *carrot* on an overhead transparency.

Discuss the fact that the child in the poem at first thought the word began with the letter *k*. Ask students to think of other examples of words that begin with the letter *c* but sound like *k*. Word suggestions could include *car, corn, cow, caterpillar, cup,* or *cub*. Write the words in a list and explain that they begin with a hard *c* sound.

> **Our Promise to Each Other**
>
> In 1-W, we promise to work together and help each other like <u>Swimmy</u> and the red fish. We will show each other that we care by sharing, speaking kindly, and using our manners. We will appreciate other people's hard work and remember that mistakes are learning opportunities. We know that it's O.K. to be unique like <u>Woolbur</u> and that our best "ISH" work is just fine. We promise to STOP when someone says STOP. This is who we are even WHEN NO ONE IS WATCHING! ☺

In her book *Reading With Meaning*, Debbie Miller suggests creating a "Classroom Promise."

- Contrast this first list with words from around the room that begin with a soft *c* like *city, circle, cylinder,* or *cent*.

- Review the word lists together, making sure students know each word. As you do, circle the vowels that follow the initial consonant.

- Ask if students can detect the rule that will help them know whether the *c* in a word is hard or soft. You may need to teach them that the *c* is hard when followed by *a, u,* or *o*. It is soft when followed by *e, i,* or *y*. Ask students to be on the lookout for these words in their reading.

Options for Differentiation: Word Sorting Tips

As a follow-up for those students who need additional hands-on practice, use the word sort on page 34. A reproducible version is provided in Appendix 1 on page 139. If this is your students' first experience sorting words, work with them in a small guided word-study group. Begin by reading all the words and checking for understanding. Then do a teacher-directed sort where you tell students the key words. In this case, the key words could be *car* and *cent*. To sort words, students cut the words apart, read each word, and place the word in a column under the key word that has the same beginning sound. After the words are sorted, cement the learning by asking students, "How are all the words in this column alike?" For added learning, once words are sorted by beginning sound, invite students to sort the words in each column by the number of syllables (Bear, Invernizzi, Templeton, & Johnson, 2007).

car	city	cereal	cow
caterpillar	centipede	cent	cup
camp	cylinder	circle	cycle
corn	cub	cookie	

WRITING

Invite students to be "convention detectives" and find the part of the poem that contains the exact words someone says. If they cannot do so, show them the clues—quotation marks. Find other examples in texts where a conversation is enclosed in quotation marks. One wonderful title is *The Perfect Nest* by Catherine Friend (2007). After reading the amusing tale, use the document camera or overhead projector to display two pages with samples of conversation. Next, model how to use quotations by writing a short, imaginary conversation between two classmates. Then, let the students try during writing workshop. Return to this lesson from time to time in the coming weeks to reinforce this often-confusing skill.

Picture Book Pairings for "The Eraser"

One (Otoshi, 2008)
A thought-provoking book about bullying.

The Recess Queen (O'Neill, 2002)
A new girl challenges Mean Jean's status as playground bully.

Mini-Lessons for "Crayons: A Rainbow Poem" by Jane Yolen

COMPREHENSION: INFERRING

This poem offers an ideal opportunity to introduce or practice the comprehension strategy of inferring. Prior to sharing the poem, cover the title. Remind students that readers infer what is happening in a story or poem by "reading between the lines." Read the poem aloud. Invite students to turn and talk to their partners about what they infer the poem is about based on the word clues from the poem and their prior knowledge. Reread the poem. Ask students to share their thinking with the class. Once your conversation is complete, reveal the title and discuss whether their thinking matched the author's idea or went in a different direction.

SIGHT VOCABULARY

To improve students' knowledge of color words, print the poem on sentence strips and place it in a pocket chart. Slip a card with a square of color in front of each color word. Then, print each color word on an index card. Chorally read the poem with the colored squares in place of color words. Next, show children

CRAYONS: A RAINBOW POEM

by Jane Yolen

This box contains the wash of blue sky,
spikes of green spring,
a circle of yellow sun,
triangle flames of orange and red.

It has a lime caterpillar
inching on a brown branch,
the shadow black in the center
of a grove of trees.

It holds my pink
and your chocolate
and her burnt sienna
and his ivory skin.

In it are all the colors of the world.
All
    the
       colors
         of
           the
             world.

Source: *Poetry Speaks to Children* (Paschen, 2005)

two options for each color from the printed cards containing the color words. For example, for the word *blue*, show children the printed cards containing *green* and *blue*. Ask them to point to the word that says *blue*. Once they've correctly identified the word, ask a child to explain how he or she figured it out (beginning sound, ending sound, middle sound). Continue in the same fashion with remaining color words. Finally, reread the poem with the words in place. Provide students with a set of color-word flash cards for continued practice.

MEANING VOCABULARY TO HIGHLIGHT FOR ELLS

Point out words with multiple meanings, such as *wash*, *spikes*, and *inching* that appear in the following phrases:

a wash of blue

spikes of green

inching along

Explain these meanings so that children begin to understand the different ways English words are used. For example, in this poem "a wash of blue" is not referring to washing your hands, and "inching along" is not telling a measurement (it is a way of describing how something moves slowly). Reinforce understanding with appropriate pictures or actions.

Picture Book Pairings for "Crayons: A Rainbow Poem"

Bein' With You This Way (Nikola-Lisa, 1994)
A rap-like ode that celebrates the beauty of diversity.

The Colors of Us (Katz, 2002)
Lena's mom helps her see that the color brown comes in many shades.

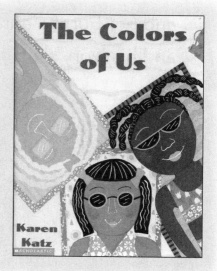

Friendship: More Poems and Mini-Lessons

"Friendship" by Risa Jordan (p. 11)

Found In: *A Poem a Day* (Moore, 1997)

Summary of Poem: The theme of this poem is that friends are special in many ways.

Phonemic Awareness: Rhyming Words

Read the poem aloud and invite students to share any rhymes that they hear. If necessary, repeat the poem a few times, offering more students a chance to listen and then identify rhymes. Next, ask children what other words they can tell you that rhyme with *well/tell, too/ you, mind/kind, far/are.*

Phonics: Differentiating Between Rimes and Rhymes

For this poem, use the activity Rounding Up the Rhymes, developed by Patricia Cunningham, the creator of the Four Blocks literacy framework (Cunningham, 2009a, pp. 128–131).

- Read the poem. We selected this particular poem because it has a lot of rhymes with the same spelling patterns.

- Round up the rhymes. As the children tell you the rhyming words, write each word on an index card and place it in the pocket chart.

- Separate the rhymes from the rimes (words with the same spelling pattern). To demonstrate the power of word families or spelling patterns, discard words that do not have the same spelling pattern.

- Apply knowledge to reading. Write a word that has the same spelling pattern as the rounded-up rhymes. Without saying the word, see if a student can put it under the rhyming word that will help them figure it out. Continue with a few more words in this fashion.

- Apply knowledge to spelling. Say a word that students might need when they are writing, and have them decide which word in the pocket chart would help them spell that word.

Fluency

Lead the way by modeling echo reading for your students. For additional practice, select two students to demonstrate how to do echo reading together. Then, assist partners as they practice in the same fashion. You may want to advise children how to choose who will be the "teacher" first. Some suggestions include choosing the person whose first initial is closest to the letter *A* or the partner who has the most letters in his or her first name.

Options for Differentiation

When working with ELLs, partner each learner with a more fluent reader for the echo reading work. Then, using the "echo" poem for inspiration, have ELLs work with a teacher's aide or upper-grade student to write a poem about a friend.

With all of the poems in this book, record them and place them in a listening center, along with copies of each poem. One poem plus a tape or CD can be placed in a labeled resealable plastic bag for easy access. Students can listen to the poems and follow along with text to strengthen word recognition and fluency. Students can also read along quietly with each poem.

Picture Book Pairings

39 Uses for a Friend (Ziefert, 2001). Brief text and simple illustrations celebrate the many ways friends help each other.

Best Friends (Kellogg, 1986). Kathy is lonely when her best friend goes to summer camp.

"When Hannah Moved Away" by Judith Viorst (p. 114)

Found In: *The Random House Book of Poetry for Children* (Prelutsky, 1983)

Summary of Poem: The days are not quite the same when a best friend moves away.

Phonics: Consonant Blends

After reading the poem aloud and enjoying it together, circle the words that contain initial consonant blends. Point out that each of these words begins with two consonants that work together as a team to begin the word, but they keep their own sounds. Slowly read the words *flat, sky, grouchy, gray, prunes, stay, flowers, smell,* and *play*. Choose two of the blends for focus work: *fl* and *gr*. Write them on the document camera or board and invite the class to contribute other words that begin with those blends. Post a chart of the completed list for easy viewing. Encourage students to be on the lookout for more words to add to the list.

Fluency

Read the poem aloud, modeling how your tone can convey the mood of the poem. Ask students to practice reading the poem with a partner, taking turns adding expression to the lines. Then, cut the poem into individual lines. Invite students to pick a line out of a container and practice reading it with expression.

Assemble the students in front of the class in the order in which their lines appear in the poem, and have them "read along the line" with expression. On another day, give the students who weren't involved last time first choice at drawing a line from a container, and repeat the process. Emphasize that reading with expression is an important part of being a fluent reader.

Writing

Invite children to share how they felt when one of their best friends moved away, and write their comments on the document camera or board. To connect with the poem, ask if the poet expresses any of those same feelings. Then, highlight the way Judith Viorst showed how the child was feeling: *cola without the fizz, pizza that tastes like cardboard, a smile turned upside down*. Ask students to work in pairs to take a happy feeling or favorite food and make it less appealing. Model with several examples of your own before the children begin. Share the final results, emphasizing that this is one way to "show" rather than "tell" something when they write.

Options for Differentiation

During guided reading, work with ELL students to ensure they understand the vocabulary in this poem and the contrasts the poet is making. Writing about chocolate ice cream that tastes like prunes will be confusing to these learners unless they understand how the author is trying to show that his or her life is not the same now that a best friend has moved. Invite students to work together to write or illustrate a similar representation of several of the examples to help clarify what the poet is attempting to do.

Picture Book Pairings

Alexander, Who's Not (Do you hear me? I mean it!) Going to Move (Viorst, 1995). Alexander doesn't want to move away and leave his favorite friends and special places.

Ira Says Goodbye (Waber, 1988). Ira's friend Reggie is moving to a new town.

Mini-Lessons for "A Family Is . . ." by Maria Walther

COMPREHENSION: BUILDING BACKGROUND KNOWLEDGE

If teaching about families is a part of your social studies instruction, use this poem to spark a discussion about what makes each child's family special.

WRITING

Using the pattern from the poem, "A Family Is. . .," invite students to make a list of all the words that tell about their family. Then have them play around with the words to arrange them into their own family poem.

Picture Book Pairings for "A Family Is . . ."

- - - - - - - - - - - - - - - - - -

The Chicken of the Family (Amato, 2008)
Henrietta's older sisters, who are always teasing her, convince her she is a chicken.

The Family Book (Parr, 2003)
In his unique and colorful way, Todd Parr delivers the message that family members' love for one another is what really matters.

A FAMILY IS . . .
by Maria Walther

A family is love,

A family is kindness,

A family's a fun place to be.

A family is caring,

A family is sharing,

My family is just right for me!

Families: More Poems and Mini-Lessons

"Brother" by Mary Ann Hoberman (p. 95)

Found In: *Poetry Speaks to Children* (Paschen, 2005)

Summary of Poem: When a child's little brother is being a bother, he brings him to his mother and father, who tell him that all little brothers are bothers.

Phonemic Awareness: Beginning Consonant Sound—/b/

Read the poem through once, just so children can enjoy the language. Next, as you reread the poem orally, ask children to clap when they hear the /b/ sound. Reread it one more time, but pick up the pace a little, so children hear how much fun this tongue twister is to read aloud!

Phonics: Word Endings—(-er)

To help students answer the question, "What two letters make the /er/ sound?" list the following -er words on the overhead or chart paper: *brother, mother, father, bother,* and *another*. Discuss and highlight the fact that the /er/ sound at the end of these words is made by writing the letters *e* and *r*. Ask the children to think of several other words that end with this sound. Write them on the board and check together to see if it is -er at work again. Challenge students to find more -er words during the week and add them to the chart. Set aside a few minutes to read through the growing collection of words.

Fluency

Read this poem through at a reasonable pace the first few times you read it. Teach children that seasoned readers adjust their rates of reading. They will read something new more slowly than they will read text they have practiced. Begin by rereading it chorally as a group, and then send students off in small groups or pairs to continue the practice. Challenge students to reread this tongue-twisting poem faster and faster. End the mini-lesson by asking for volunteers to reread the poem to the class. Encourage them to take a copy of the poem home and read it to someone in their family for extra practice.

Picture Book Pairings

My Brother (Browne, 2007). A young boy tells all the cool things about his older brother.

Oh, Brother (Grimes, 2008). In 20 related poems, Grimes captures the struggles Xavier faces when his mother remarries and his stepbrother Chris moves in to his home.

"My Sister Is a Sissy" by Jack Prelutsky (p. 138)

Found In: *The New Kid on the Block* (Prelutsky, 1984)

Summary of Poem: A sibling tells about all the things that make his or her sister scared.

Phonics: "is" Contractions

The word *she's* appears in the poem a number of times, providing the opportunity to introduce or review "is" contractions such as *she's, he's, it's, that's, who's, what's, where's, when's, why's,* and *how's*.

Meaning Vocabulary: Synonyms

In this poem, Prelutsky uses the synonyms *afraid, terrified,* and *scared* to describe the way the sister feels. Build on these words by creating a word web of all the different ways writers can say *scared*. Post the web in your room for future reference.

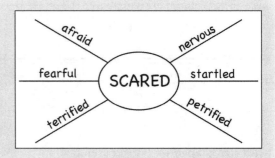

Picture Book Pairings

Scaredy Squirrel (Watt, 2008). As the title suggests, Scaredy Squirrel is afraid of everything.

There's a Big, Beautiful World Out There! (Carlson, 2002). A young girl discovers all the beauty in our frequently scary world.

| POETIC PICTURE BOOKS AND THEMED ANTHOLOGIES ||
Title	Brief Summary
Almost Late to School: And Other School Poems (Diggory Shields, 2003)	Events that are a part of an elementary school day are amusingly portrayed to delight readers.
Bats at the Library (Lies, 2008)	A colony of bats reads, plays, and acts out bits of favorite classics during their night at the library.
Best Friends (Hopkins, 1986)	Numerous poems share the ups and downs of friendship.
Black Is Brown Is Tan (Adoff, 1973)	Members of an interracial family are celebrated through verse.
Born to Read (Sierra, 2008)	Determined to win a bicycle, Sam reads everything he can to achieve his goal.
Danitra Brown, Class Clown (Grimes, 2005)	A series of rhyming poems tells the story of Danitra and her friend Zuri starting a new school year.
In Daddy's Arms, I Am Tall (Steptoe, 1997)	This collection celebrates African American fathers.
Night on Neighborhood Street (Greenfield, 1991)	Poems depict daily life in an African American neighborhood.
School Supplies (Hopkins, 1996)	This anthology brings school tools to life with a fresh perspective on such things as the school bus, pencils, and paper clips.
Vacation: We're Going to the Ocean (Harrison, 2009)	A young boy's beach vacation is filled with fun and surprises.

Playful Phonemic Awareness Activities

Translating Research Into Sensible Daily Practice

Experts in the field identify phonemic awareness as an essential building block for learning to read (Yopp & Yopp, 2000). In fact, the level of phonemic awareness children have when entering school is widely held to be the single strongest determinant of how easily and successfully they'll learn to read. Fortunately for children who enter school lacking these skills, research clearly shows that phonemic awareness can be developed through instruction and, furthermore, that doing so significantly boosts students' subsequent reading and writing achievement (Adams, 1990; Stanovich, 1986). Wow! That's about all there is to say about this statement. If you've been working with young readers for any length of time, you know that a lack of phonemic awareness hinders their progress as readers.

What does research tell us about sensible ways to make phonemic awareness development a part of our everyday core literacy instruction? To begin, make time each day for your students to write using their own developing spelling skills. Studies have shown that primary teachers who promote early writing activities by encouraging students to use developmental spelling and by demonstrating for their young learners how to stretch out the sounds in words while they compose morning messages or engage in interactive writing lessons see a growth in students' ability to segment phonemes (McGill-Franzen, Allington, Yokoi, & Brooks, 1999; Scanlon & Vellutino, 1997). In addition to daily writing, your phonemic awareness instruction should consist of developmentally appropriate activities that are engaging, interactive, and social and that develop students' curiosity about and desire to experiment with the sounds of language (Yopp, 1992).

PHONEMIC AWARENESS SKILLS TO HIGHLIGHT THROUGH POETRY	
Phonemic Awareness Skills (in order of difficulty)	**Ideas for Language Play With Poetry**
Language Awareness	After reading and rereading poems, invite students to do the following: • Echo or repeat lines or phrases from the poem. • Clap the words in a line of poetry, and then count the words in that particular line. • Clap the syllables in a line of poetry, and then count the syllables in that particular line.
Rhyming	After enjoying a rhyming poem, choose one or more of these options: • Ask listeners if they heard any rhyming words. • Call out a series of three words from the poem (two that rhyme, one that doesn't), and ask students to identify the rhyming pair or the non-rhyming word. • Target one rhyming word pair from the poem and invite children to produce as many words as they can that rhyme with the selected rhyming pair.
Identify Initial Phonemes/ Sounds (Onsets)	• If a poem features alliteration, repeat the alliterative line or phrase; invite students to isolate and identify the beginning sound.
Blending	• If a poem contains compound words, say the two individual words and ask children to blend them together to state the compound word. • If the poem has multisyllabic words, pronounce the separate syllables in a word and invite students to blend them together to state the whole word. • Choose three or four c-v-c (consonant, short vowel, consonant) words, such as *bat, pet, win, rob,* or *sun,* from the poem. Say the onset (initial phoneme/sound) and the rime (final phoneme/sound)—for example, /b/ . . . -at—and invite listeners to blend the parts together and verbalize the whole word (*bat*). • Pick three or four longer words from the poem, say the individual phonemes, and invite young learners to blend the phonemes together to say the whole word—children enjoy testing their skills on longer words. To promote careful listening, pause for a few seconds between each phoneme.
Segmenting	• Isolate a line or phrase from the poem. Invite students to stand up and repeat the line or phrase—jumping, marching, or tiptoeing one time for each word. Follow the same procedure for segmenting the individual words in compound words or the syllables in a multisyllabic spoken word. • Select three or four c-v-c (consonant, short vowel, consonant) words, such as *bat, pet, win, rob, sun,* from the poem. Say the whole word and invite listeners to segment the onset (beginning phoneme/sound) and the rime (ending phoneme/sound). • Choose three or four longer words from the poem, say the whole word, and invite young learners to segment the phonemes contained in the whole word.
Substituting Phonemes	• Play the substitution game. Select a word, such as *ran,* from the poem. Instruct the students to repeat *ran.* Then say, "Delete the *r,* add a *t,* and tell me what you hear." Students reply, "Tan."
Adding Phonemes	• Choose compound words from the poem, such as *airplane.* Say "Air + plane = ___?" Students reply, "Airplane." • Follow the same procedure to add syllables together to create multisyllabic words, and to add onsets to rimes, or vice versa.
Deleting Phonemes	• Select a line or phrase from the poem, such as "Fun for you and fun for me." Recite the line, and have students repeat. Then say, "Repeat the line again without the word *you,* and replace the word with a clap." Students repeat, "Fun for [clap] and fun for me." • Choose compound words from the poem, such as *doghouse.* Say "doghouse," and have students echo back "doghouse." Then say, "The word *doghouse* without *dog* is _____ [house]." Continue with other compound words. • Follow the same procedure for multisyllabic words, deleting phonemes from the beginning, middle, or end of words.

CHAPTER 3
ADVENTURE!
ANIMAL POEMS

Explore the Animal World

Grab your binoculars and climb aboard. Let's take students on an animal adventure! In selecting the poems for this chapter, we thought about our struggling and reluctant readers. What kinds of animals appeal to them? When asked, one of Maria's students replied, "Anything ocean!" If your students are also curious to learn about creatures of the deep, you'll find poems featuring fierce sharks and gigantic whales. Other readers might be more interested in slithery snakes of any kind, and, of course, there are those students who can't pass up a book or poem about their favorite pet. We're hopeful that you will find selections that entice even your most resistant readers to explore the animal world through the carefully crafted words of a poem.

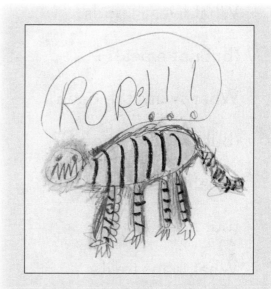

Tigers are terrible
Tigers are tough
Tigers are really, really buff

Written by: Aleksandar Schroeder

Mini-Lessons for "Guess" by Eileen Spinelli

COMPREHENSION: INFERRING

Display "Guess" without showing the last line. Remind students that thoughtful readers infer as they are reading to try and figure out what is happening in the poem or, in this case, what the poem is about.

GUESS

by Eileen Spinelli

What's black and white

(but not a penguin)?

What's fast and fierce

(but not a bear)?

What lives in pods

(but not a pea)?

What swims the deep

(but breathes the air)?

What eats a lot

(but not a hog)?

What leaps to life

(but not a quail)?

What has sharp teeth

(but not a shark)?

Answer, please:

The killer whale.

Source: *Polar Bear, Arctic Hare* (Spinelli, 2007)

Discuss how the poet, Eileen Spinelli, chose to write her poem as a guessing game. As you chorally read this poem with your students, invite them to share their inferences based on the clues from the poem and their schema or prior knowledge. You might consider charting students' ideas as you think about and discuss the clues in the poem. See sample chart below.

THOUGHTFUL READERS INFER AS THEY READ		
Clues	Schema	Revised Thinking
black and white	Other black and white animals I've seen: panda, whale, skunk	N/A
swims the deep	I know oceans are deep	It can't be a panda or skunk, because they don't swim

To reinforce the importance of using clues from the author's words coupled with schema or prior knowledge to infer, repeat this mini-lesson during guided reading with a text at your students' instructional level.

MEANING VOCABULARY: "THREE READ-ALOUD WORDS"

Use the strategy "Three Read-Aloud Words" (Cunningham, 2009b) from page 26 to target the words *fierce*, *breathes*, and *leaps* found in the poem "Guess."

MEANING VOCABULARY TO HIGHLIGHT FOR ELLS

Two words in this poem have multiple meanings—*hog* and *pod*. Multiple-meaning words are challenging for ELLs. To introduce or reinforce the concept that many words in the English language have multiple meanings, begin with the familiar word *play*. Show learners visuals of children playing, a stage play, and a child playing a musical instrument. Discuss the different meanings of the word *play*. Then, reread the poem and highlight the words *hog* and *pod*. Again, display visuals of a *hog* (the animal) and someone *hogging* the toys. Ask the children to match the meaning of the word in the poem to the visual. Repeat with the word *pod*.

Picture Book Pairings for "Guess"

Peggony-Po: A Whale of a Tale (Pinkney, 2006)
A wooden boy promises to catch the whale that bit off his daddy's leg.

The Snail and the Whale (Donaldson, 2003)
A rhyming tale about a snail who hitches a ride with a whale and ends up saving him when he gets stranded on a beach.

Ocean Animals: More Poems and Mini-Lessons

"The Shark" by Lord Alfred Douglas (p. 78)

Found In: *The Random House Book of Poetry* (Prelutsky, 1983)

Summary of Poem: The treacherous shark waits patiently for a person to get into the water.

Phonemic Awareness: Syllables

Once you've read "The Shark" for pleasure, select a variety of one-, two-, or three-syllable words from the poem. Invite students to clap the syllables as you say each word aloud. To extend the learning in the days to come, ensure that each student knows how many syllables are in his or her first name. At different times during the day, dismiss students by the number of syllables in their first name by saying, "If you have a one-syllable name, you may get ready for lunch," and so on.

Suggested Words:
- one-syllable words: *shark, bite, fish*
- two-syllable words: *monster, body, stomach*
- three-syllable words: *appealing, excitement, dangerous*

Comprehension: Comparing Texts About the Same Topic

Pair this poem with a nonfiction title about sharks such as *Sharks!* (Schreiber, 2008) to compare and contrast the two genres. Discuss and note the differences in the two types of texts.

Meaning Vocabulary: Synonyms

Highlight the following three words on the document camera or an overhead transparency: *treacherous, astounding,* and *demeanor.* Pronounce each word and share a child-friendly definition—an explanation that is more easily understood than those often offered by a dictionary (Beck, McKeown & Kucan, 2008). For example, you might say that *treacherous* refers to something unsafe or extremely dangerous, such as rock climbing. Then, ask children to work in triads to come up with two synonyms for each word. Some examples might include these:
- *treacherous*: dangerous, perilous, hazardous, risky, unsafe
- *astounding*: surprising, shocking, amazing, astonishing
- *demeanor*: manner, behavior, conduct, character

Ask students to share their synonyms for each word in a sentence to help the class understand how they could use that word in their writing. Post a chart of these vocabulary words and their synonyms for future writing use.

Picture Book Pairings

Don't Eat the Teacher! (Ward, 2002). It's Sammy the Shark's first day of school and he has a little problem—he eats everything in sight!

All About Sharks (Arnosky, 2003). This nonfiction book contains fascinating information about a variety of different kinds of sharks.

"Whale" by Mary Ann Hoberman (p. 57)

Found In: *The Llama Who Had No Pajama: 100 Favorite Poems* (Hoberman, 1998)

Summary of Poem: A whale is satisfied just the way he is—stout, enormous, and chubby.

Fluency

This poem is easily divided for a small-group Readers Theater performance or for reading aloud with two voices. There are five stanzas, each with four lines. We would suggest that for each stanza, one group or individual reads the first two lines and another group or individual reads the second two lines. The final stanza can be read in unison. Provide students with ample time to practice before performing for their peers.

Comprehension: Thinking About Characters

The whale in this poem has a strong sense of self. After reading the poem, ask the students to notice what the whale thinks and does in the poem. Discuss how clues such as these help readers learn what is important to that character. Continue this conversation during read-aloud or guided reading with other stories that have strong characters.

Sight Vocabulary: Family Word Bingo

The words *family* and *friends* along with other "family" words such as *daughters* and *sons* appear in this poem and in many stories that students will read. Take this opportunity to focus on family words by playing a quick game of word bingo. To get ready to play, students draw a tic-tac-toe board on a piece of paper, then write a "family" word in each space. See suggested words at right. As you call out words, students cover the corresponding word with a chip or marker of some kind.

mother	father	sister
brother	son	family
grandma	grandpa	daughter
aunt	uncle	cousin

Options for Differentiation

To help ELLs make personal connections with each family word, students might write in the names of family members or draw a picture of that person under each word on their bingo card.

Picture Book Pairings

Whales Passing (Bunting, 2003). A father and son have a conversation as they watch a pod of orcas swim and play.

A Garden of Whales (Davis, 2008). A young boy's imagination takes him into the mysterious world of whales.

A RUMBA OF RATTLESNAKES

by Marjorie Maddox

A rumba of rattlesnakes knows how to shake

their long, slinky bodies and twist till daybreak.

They wobble their heads, give their hips a quick quake.

They jitterbug tails till their skeletons ache.

They rattle maracas and *rat-tat* on drums,

blow on tin trumpets, uncurl their tongues

to hiss a sweet song that invites you to come

a little bit closer. But you know to run

way over here to avoid the mistake

of dancing the rumba with ten rattlesnakes.

Source: *A Crossing of Zebras: Animal Packs in Poetry* (Maddox, 2008)

Mini-Lessons for "A Rumba of Rattlesnakes" by Marjorie Maddox

PHONEMIC AWARENESS: ALLITERATION

This poem offers an opportunity to listen for and highlight the poet's use of alliteration, or the repetition of the beginning sound with phrases like "quick quake," "tin trumpets," and "sweet song." Play an alliteration game by inviting students to think of a word that begins with the same letter as their name, such as *Lenny's lemons*, *Stephanie's snakes*, *Tony's trumpets*, or *Katie's kites*. Sit in a circle and ask each student to share his or her alliteration. If time permits, students can draw an illustration to accompany their alliteration.

FLUENCY

Once students hear, read, and chorally practice "A Rumba of Rattlesnakes" a number of times, they will be begging to perform it. If you have a music program in your building, borrow a few maracas and some small drums or rhythm sticks. If not, ask the children to think of items in your classroom that would simulate the sounds found in the poem. For example, performers can pretend to play trumpets and create their own hissing sounds. Once you've gathered the instruments, divide students into two groups—an "acting" group and a "playing" group. Next, within those groups assign partners or triads a line of the poem to rehearse and perform. Circulate and assist individual readers as needed. Once the groups are ready, perform! Use the video mode on a digital camera to capture a quick video of your budding stars.

MEANING VOCABULARY: VERBS

Write each of the following verbs on a separate index card: *shake, twist, wobble, rattle,* and *uncurl.* Play "charades" by selecting a student to act out the verb without using sounds while the rest of the class attempts to guess the verb.

Picture Book Pairings for "A Rumba of Rattlesnakes"

Baby Rattlesnake/Viborita de Cascabel (Ata, 2003)
Baby Rattlesnake learns a valuable lesson when he misuses his rattle.

Count on Culebra: Go from 1 to 10 in Spanish (Paul, 2008)
Culebra (snake) and friends help Iguana make her famous cactus-butter candies.

Desert Animals: More Poems and Mini-Lessons

"The Lizard" by John Gardner (p. 45)

Found In: *Eric Carle's Animals, Animals* (1989)

Summary of Poem: A four-line poem about a lizard who longs to be a dinosaur.

Phonics: Word Families (-ing)

Highlight the words *thing* and *sing* in "The Lizard." Draw students' attention to the fact that both words belong to the *-ing* word family. Send students on an *-ing* word hunt through a familiar book or a poem in their poetry binder. Once they have collected five or six words, use the words in a sort. Sort by number of syllables. Then re-sort by whether the *-ing* is part of the word, as in *sing*, or is a word ending, as in *jumping*. Point out that the letters sound the same no matter which role they play.

Meaning Vocabulary: An Alphabet of Action Verbs

Gardner's poem includes the verbs *dance, fly, sing,* and *hunt.* Use these verbs as a starting point for creating an alphabet of action verbs. Print each of the words at right on an index card. Use the action cards to play charades by having a child select a card and act out the verb.

bounce	hunt	nip	vacuum
crawl	juggle	paint	walk
dance	kick	run	yawn
fly	leap	sing	yell
grin	march	talk	zip

Picture Book Pairings

Desert Song (Johnston, 2000). The sights and sounds of the desert are unveiled through rhythmic text and striking illustrations.

Way Out in the Desert (Marsh, 1999). Patterned after "Over in the Meadow," this poem helps children learn about many animal families that live in the desert.

"The Coyote" by Douglas Florian (p. 13)

Found In: *Mammalabilia* (Florian, 2000)

Summary of Poem: A coyote prowls, howls, and loves the long vowel o.

Phonics: Word Sort /owl/ vs. /own/

The words *prowl, growl,* and *howl,* found in "The Coy-ote," all have the same spelling pattern—/owl/. To explore the difference between words with the /owl/ pattern and the /own/ pattern, students can complete the word sort of the words listed on page 53. A reproducible version is provided on page 140 in the appendix.

For word sorting tips, see page 33.

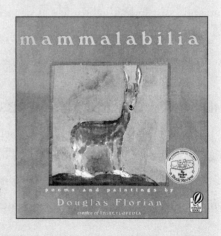

down	gown	prowl	scowl
growl	town	howl	brown
fowl	clown	crown	jowl

Writing

To guide students as they write a free-verse poem about an animal of their choice, demonstrate how to make a list of all of the things an animal does. For example, if you were going to model writing a poem about a cow, you might list the following words and phrases:

moos
makes milk
swishes her tail
chews

Next, demonstrate how poets play with the words until they've created a poem.

"The Cow"
I moo.
I chew.
I make milk for you.
For I am a cow.

Encourage students to try this on their own during writing workshop. Provide additional support to those who need it.

Picture Book Pairings

A Desert Scrapbook: Dawn to Dusk in the Sonoran Desert (Wright-Frierson, 1996). While carefully observing desert life, the author creates a scrapbook with her sketches and notes.

Coyote: A Trickster Tale From the American Southwest (McDermott, 1994). Coyote's dream to fly like the crows ends in a memorable lesson.

Mini-Lessons for "I Would Like to Have a Pet" by Karla Kuskin

PHONICS: WORD FAMILIES (-ALL)

Reread the poem and highlight the words with the *-all* spelling pattern. Tell students that you are going to play a word family game called "Roll the Ball." To play this fun phonics game, you will need to get a ball from the P. E. teacher. Sit in a circle with your students. Say the word *ball* and then roll the ball to a student. That child says a word that rhymes with *ball* and then rolls the ball to another learner. The

Moon, Have You Met My Mother?
The collected poems of Karla Kuskin

Illustrations by Sergio Ruzzier

I WOULD LIKE TO HAVE A PET
by Karla Kuskin

I would like to have a pet

any kind at all.

Something big,

something small,

something sleeping in the hall

would be just fine.

I would like to have a pet.

Will you be mine?

Source: *Moon, Have You Met My Mother? The Collected Poems of Karla Kuskin* (Kuskin, 2003)

play continues in this fashion. After the game, invite students to work with a friend to write a list of as many *-all* family words as they can think of. Compile the lists into one chart to display for future reference.

COMPREHENSION: ACTIVATING SCHEMA

To activate students' schema or background knowledge about pets, prepare a set of picture cards of various pets. Work with students to sort these pictures in different ways. Begin with big pets and small pets. Next, ask learners to decide two different features that they could use to sort the picture cards.

Options for Differentiation

The same picture cards would be a handy resource for ELLs who aren't familiar with the names of common household pets. Use the cards during guided reading to have students name the pets. Then, add another set of cards with the animals' names (*cat, dog, hamster*, and so on) printed on them. Students can match the pet picture with the pet name in a literacy center or during an independent practice time.

WRITING

Discuss the different traits that students would look for in a pet. Remind them that it could be a real pet or an imaginary pet. In a shared writing format, compose a class poem using Kuskin's pattern. If students choose, they can write and illustrate their own poem during writing workshop.

I would like to have a pet
any kind at all.
Something _____,
something _____,
something _____
would be just fine.
I would like to have a pet.
Will you be mine?

Picture Book Pairings for "I Would Like to Have a Pet"

Can I Keep Him? (Kellogg, 1971)
Arnold's mother says no to every pet he wants . . . well, almost!

What Pet to Get? (Dodd, 2008)
Jack has a lot of ideas for pets such as a *T. rex* or an elephant, but with gentle nudging from his mother, he ends up with a puppy.

Pets: More Poems and Mini-Lessons

"The Monster's Pet" by Lilian Moore (unpaged)

Found In: *Beware, Take Care: Fun and Spooky Poems by Lilian Moore* (Moore, 2006)

Summary of Poem: Ponders the possibilities of the kind of pet a monster might choose.

Phonemic Awareness: Playing With Nonsense Words

Poems like "The Monster's Pet" manipulate language in a playful way, encouraging students to chime in as you read aloud. If your students enjoy the word play in this poem, you can also share "The Yak" by Jack Prelutsky, found in his book *Zoo Doings* (1983).

Phonics: Word Families—(-et)

Use the words *get, pet,* and *set* to begin a phonics lesson on the *-et* word family.

Sight Vocabulary

The sight word *would* is repeated five times in this poem, making it ideal for repeated reading with an emphasis on that word.

Picture Book Pairings

When a Monster Was Born (Taylor, 2007). A humorous circular story about a monster.

Where the Wild Things Are (Sendak, 1988). When Max is sent to his room for misbehaving, he travels to an island to become king of the wild things.

"Wishes" by Susan Pearson (p. 5)

Found In: *Who Swallowed Harold?* (Pearson, 2005)

Summary of Poem: This poem details all the different things a child does to prepare for various kinds of pets.

Meaning Vocabulary: Compound Words

The poem "Wishes" contains the compound words *dog-house, without, fishbowl,* and *birdcage,* which can lead to a discussion on how readers examine word parts in an effort to figure out the whole word.

Writing

This poem is written from a first-person point of view. Reread the poem from a writer's perspective and discuss why students think Susan Pearson decided to write the poem that way. Locate other poems or picture books written in first-person point of view to read aloud.

Picture Book Pairings

Hi! Fly Guy (Arnold, 2006). Buzz enters his pet fly in The Amazing Pet Show.

Duck and Cover (Urbanovic, 2009). Harold the alligator visits Irene and her friends because he thinks he's eaten someone's pet.

POETIC PICTURE BOOKS AND THEMED ANTHOLOGIES	
Title	**Brief Summary**
Bees, Snails, & Peacock Tails (Franco, 2008)	These poems describe the patterns and shapes found in nature.
Commotion in the Ocean (Andreae, 1998)	If your students love ocean animals, you have to have this book.
Dinosaurs Galore! (Andreae, 2005)	You'll meet a dozen different dinosaurs in this rhyming picture book.
Dinothesaurus (Florian, 2009)	Dinosaur fans can learn about 18 different kinds of dinosaurs, along with how to pronounce their names, while reading these engaging poems.
Mammalabilia (Florian, 2000)	This collection of short poems about mammals includes an aardvark, an otter, a hippo, and a host of others.
Once I Ate a Pie (MacLachlan & Charest, 2006)	The poetic tales of 13 different dogs are each written in free verse with creative uses of font sizes and word placement.
Rumble in the Jungle (Andreae, 1996)	Jungle animals are introduced in rhyming verses.
Squeal and Squawk: Barnyard Talk (Pearson, 2004)	Pearson has created fresh and funny poems about farm animals.
There Was a Coyote Who Swallowed a Flea (Ward, 2006)	A hungry coyote gobbles down everything in sight in this funny tale.
A Whiff of Pine, A Hint of Skunk: A Forest of Poems (Ruddell, 2009)	The creators of *Today at the Bluebird Café* (2007) team up again to share a collection of poems about woodland creatures that beg to be read aloud again and again.

Explicit Phonics Lessons

Translating Research Into Sensible Daily Practice

Phonics here, phonics there, phonics conversations are happening everywhere! If you are teaching young readers how to recognize words and encouraging budding authors to write their ideas using their developmental spelling skills, chances are discussions about letters and sounds are permeating your daily instruction. Whether you are pointing out alliteration in a poem, coaching a reader as she applies decoding strategies, or demonstrating how writers use word families to help them spell words, you are, in fact, teaching phonics. If you are thinking that some of those examples sound like spelling lessons, you're right. That is because both phonics and spelling involve readers and writers in using, analyzing, and solving words—the two are interrelated. In fact, "spelling knowledge is the engine that drives efficient reading as well as writing" (Templeton & Morris, 1999, p. 103). It is through learning to spell that children internalize the alphabetic system of writing. This understanding is necessary for a learner to be able to encode words for writing and decode words for reading.

Did you know that only about half of the words in the English language are phonetically regular? Thus, in addition to phonics lessons, readers need a wide range of language knowledge and strategies to figure out unknown words (Pinnell & Fountas, 1998). While it is important that students have explicit phonics instruction within a systematic curriculum, they also benefit from hands-on activities designed to help them manipulate word features and generalize these features to entire groups of words that work the same way (Bear et al., 2007). Finally, research does *not* suggest that word recognition and decoding need to be in place before comprehension instruction occurs. In fact, comprehension instruction and instruction in word recognition and decoding can—and should—occur side by side (Stahl, 2004).

How does this translate into daily practice? As we teach, we look for ways to highlight the reciprocal relationships among spelling, writing, and reading instruction (Gentry, 2004). In addition to explicit phonics lessons and word study activities like the ones found on page 59, children learn about words through their interactions with meaningful texts such as poems. These interactions occur across the curriculum. We engage in phonics discussions while reading a morning message, singing a song about fossils, sorting words during guided reading, conferring with readers, and so on. Phonics is EVERYWHERE!

WORD STUDY IDEAS TO STRENGTHEN STUDENTS' PHONICS KNOWLEDGE	
Word Families	Reading rhyming poetry is one way to build both phonics knowledge and reading fluency (Rasinski, Rupley, & Nichols, 2008). Poems that rhyme typically contain words from a common word family, making them an ideal text for identifying and working with rimes. As you select poems, look for those containing word families that are the most common, based on frequency (Fry, 1998). (See examples, below.) Then, you can work with them in the ways listed in this chart. <table><tr><td>-ay (26 words)</td><td>-ill (26 words)</td><td>-ip (22 words)</td><td>-at (19 words)</td></tr><tr><td>-am (19 words)</td><td>-ag (19 words)</td><td>-ack (19 words)</td><td>-ank (19 words)</td></tr><tr><td>-ick (19 words)</td><td>-ell (18 words)</td><td>-ot (18 words)</td><td>-ing (18 words)</td></tr></table>
Word Sorts	When a poem contains two word families that you want to highlight, children can sort word cards according to these common word families. Another way to sort words is to give each child a small wipe-off board. Show students how to divide the board in half the long way and label each side with a word family. Then, dictate words from each word family and have them write the word on the correct side of the board. For an added challenge, dictate words that do not fit with either family.
Making Words	"Making Words" (Cunningham & Cunningham, 1992) is a multilevel activity that helps struggling readers strengthen their understanding of letter-sound relationships and learn how to look for patterns in words. To prepare a making-words lesson, target a key word from the poem that is about seven to nine letters long and create a list of small words contained in the big word. Then, provide each student with a reproducible set of letters or letter tiles. Guide students as they use the letters to make the different small words. Finally, ask them to use all the letters to make the mystery word. After making words, go back and sort the words and then apply the learning to reading and writing situations.
Word Hunts	Choose a poem, song, or story that contains many words with the phonics element you are introducing or reviewing. Do a shared reading of an enlarged copy of the poem, then invite students to circle or highlight the words containing the phonics element on their own personal copy of the poem. To collect words on a chart for future reference, ask students to share their findings.
Word Wall	A word wall is a space in your classroom that is easily seen by all students where you post *and practice* high-frequency words that are not pronounced or spelled in predictable ways. When readers know these words, it frees their attention to decipher and spell less-frequent words and to focus on the meaning of the text while they are reading. Before placing words on the wall, practice them using a variety of learning modes, such as chanting and acting out. Daily practice using different activities will help students read and spell them automatically. Holding learners accountable for correctly spelling these words in their daily writing is vital. In addition, use visuals and child-friendly definitions to help children associate meaning with words.
Word Games	To enhance your word study instruction, a wealth of commercially produced word games such as Boggle Jr., Scrabble Jr., and Scattergories is available, along with games like Word Bingo that you can make for your students.

CHAPTER 4

PERFORM!
PLAYING WITH POEMS

Lights, Camera, Action!

Some poems are calm, informative, or reflective. Others beg to be read aloud with exuberance and accompanying movements. The sampling of poems in this chapter is especially fun to read aloud and perform. You may need a collection of the lower-key poems just to settle everyone down after they participate in an energetic Readers Theater production or a rousing class rendition of a favor selection. Try *Song of the Water Boatman* (2005) or *Butterfly Eyes and Other Secrets of the Meadow* (2006), both by Joyce Sidman, for more tranquil poems. They, too, are welcome possibilities for performing. The bonus of all of this fun is that "putting on poetry" is a motivating way to strengthen fluency as children read and reread to polish their parts before sharing with an audience.

SHOUT
by Brod Bagert

Shout it! Shout it! POETRY!
Fun for you and fun for me.

Clap your hands! Stomp your feet!
Feel the rhythm! Feel the beat!

Chunky words all chopped in chips!
Silky sounds upon your lips.

Tell a story—happy, sad;
Silly, sorry; good or bad.

Leap a leap, hop a hop,
See the ocean in one drop.

Shout it! Shout it! POETRY!
Fun for you and fun for me.

Source: *Shout! Little Poems That Roar* (Bagert, 2007)

Mini-Lessons for "Shout" by Brod Bagert

FLUENCY

The poem "Shout" offers appealing performance options. First, read the poem aloud. Then, reread it two lines at a time with students echoing the lines. Finally, reread it again with the class joining in chorally. By then, children will be restraining their wiggles (or not!), wanting to act out the words. Discuss the kinds of actions that could be added to each line. To prepare "scripts" for Readers Theater, enlarge the reproducible poem on a copy machine. Cut apart into single or double lines and paste on strips of tagboard or recycled file folders. Assign lines to students in pairs or triads, grouping children so everyone gets involved and feels confident when reading aloud. Practice. Perform in class and elsewhere to spread the joy of poetry.

Options for Differentiation

Support ELLs and other students who need a boost by working individually with them on their parts during guided reading. Monitor their fluency and understanding. For continued practice, ELLs can work with a classmate who has more mastery of English to help with the pronunciation and phrasing. Students from an upper grade would also make helpful tutors. Working in pairs or small groups is a supportive way to help ELLs gain confidence in the use of language.

MEANING VOCABULARY: WORD BANKS

This poem offers interesting words such as *stomp*, *chunky*, and *silky* to extend students' vocabulary and to add to their word banks. Follow a process like this when introducing new words.

- First, guide students as they reread the poem to see if the poet gives them any clues to the meaning of the words. Gather and record their suggestions. Remind students that this process involves using the context, a handy skill for figuring out unfamiliar words.
- Revisit each word. If needed, provide a child-friendly definition. To make connections with new words, invite students to apply them to their lives. For example, have they ever *stomped* on something or felt something that was *silky*? Share experiences.
- If students don't already have word banks, show them how to create entries. First, students print each word on a 3-by-5-inch index card and punch a hole near the upper corner. For easy storage, slide words onto a binder ring. If binder rings aren't available, store word cards in a resealable plastic bag. Work with this growing stack of vocabulary cards during guided reading. Try a word sort

where students sort their words by categories, such as words with consonant blends, words with a certain vowel sound, words from a specific word family, words that contain little words, and so forth. Practice facilitates making the words a permanent part of each learner's vocabulary.

WRITING

Teach students about alliteration, a technique that poets use as they play with the sounds of language. Alliteration is the repetition of the initial consonant sound or of initial consonant blends in words that are in close proximity to one another. Point out the line in the poem that reads, "*Ch*unky words all *ch*opped in *ch*ips!" Have the students repeat it several times. Watch them smile as they play with those words. Then, read and listen to the *s* sound repeated in the lines,

> Tell a story—happy, sad;
> Silly, sorry; good or bad.

Now, pick a popular topic and demonstrate how to write an alliterative sentence. Then, write a few more in a shared writing format. Finally, give the children a chance to practice, working with partners to write their own alliterative sentences. Invite students to add this poetic element in their own poetry.

Picture Book Pairings for "Shout"

There Is a Flower at the Tip of My Nose Smelling Me (Walker, 2006)
This colorful book offers a poetic celebration of the natural world.

Will You Read to Me? (Cazet, 2007)
Hamlet the pig loves to read books and write poetry.

Playful Poetry: More Poems and Mini-Lessons

"Jump or Jiggle" by Evelyn Beyer (p. 70)

Found In: *Read-Aloud Rhymes for the Very Young* (Prelutsky, 1986)

Summary of Poem: Creatures' movements are described in rhyming couplets.

Phonemic Awareness: Rhyming Versus Non-Rhyming Words

Make a list of phrases that resemble the ones found in the poem but don't rhyme, such as these:

> Frogs hop/Caterpillars crawl
> Worms dig/Bugs sting
> Rabbits jump/Horses gallop

Read the poem aloud and invite students to listen for the rhyming words. Alternate reading phrases from the poem and the non-rhyming phrases that you created and invite students to play "thumbs up/thumbs down." If the phrase rhymes, they will put their thumbs up; if it doesn't rhyme, they indicate that by putting their thumbs down.

Meaning Vocabulary: Action Verbs

Highlight all of the verbs that show some type of action. To check understanding, ask students to tell you what each one means. Discuss how action verbs can tell what someone is doing. Then, with cautions to keep it under control, act out the words as you read the poem chorally. You might want to move this phase out to the playground!

Writing

This poem is about animals and the movements they make. Using Evelyn Beyer's poem as a pattern, change it to animals and the sounds they make in a shared writing activity. Scaffold the work by picking an animal and asking students to complete the rhyme.

> Dogs growl,
> Wolves ____ (howl).
>
> Robins cheep,
> Baby chicks ____ (peep).
>
> Owls whooo,
> Cows ____ (moo).
>
> Hens squawk,
> But I ____ (talk).

Print copies of this version for children to add to their poetry binders.

Options for Differentiation

Make illustrated vocabulary cards for ELLs with a picture of the animal on one side and the printed sound it makes on the other. Provide time for students to review the cards with a classmate or teacher's helper to aid these learners in making the necessary connections.

Picture Book Pairings

The Animal Boogie (Harter, 2000). Sing and dance your way through the jungle with animals that feel the beat.

Beetle Bop (Fleming, 2007). Fleming's rhyming text and colorful illustrations describe beetles of all shapes and sizes.

"Chant of the Awakening Bulldozers" by Patricia Hubbell (p. 6)

Found In: *Click, Rumble, Roar: Poems About Machines* (Hopkins, 1987)

Summary of the Poem: Mighty bulldozers raise their voices in a demand to be freed from their human operators.

Fluency

This poem is ideal for teaching students to use the intonation in their voices to interpret the wording of a poem. Read it through to model how you would use your voice to demonstrate the awakening bulldozers, their strength, and their demand to be

Click, Rumble, Roar

Poems About Machines

Poems selected by Lee Bennett Hopkins Photographs by Anna Held Audette

set free. Point out how the words printed in all capital letters are clues that signal children to raise their voices as they read aloud. Note that the tone is demanding and strong. Then, read the poem chorally. You might have to close the classroom door for this part! Group students into pairs or triads to practice the words, the expression, and a few gestures. Present in small groups representing a collection of bulldozers' voices.

Meaning Vocabulary

Select *puny*, *blades*, *treads*, and *evolving*. Using a picture of a bulldozer, show the blades and treads so all students have a clear picture of what they are. Give child-friendly definitions for *puny* and *evolving*. For example:

> *puny*: something that is small and weak
> *evolving*: something that is developing or changing

Connect these words to other things the students suggest that are puny or that evolve. This step ties new words to existing words in the students' schema. Slip new words into directions, class examples, and conversations from time to time to increase exposure to any new vocabulary.

Writing

Model the use of first-person voice by writing two poems from the perspective of familiar objects such as a tennis shoe, a backpack, or the classroom computer. Compose a poem that sounds demanding and another that is friendlier in tone. Invite students to pick an inanimate object and write a poem from that object's point of view. Polish and compile poems in a class book titled *Voices, Voices Everywhere*.

Picture Book Pairings

Trucks and Earthmovers (Graham, 2006). Children will pore over this book about fascinating machines.

My Truck Is Stuck! (Lewis, 2002). In this rhyming story, the driver of a dump truck stuck in a pothole has trouble getting help.

Mini-Lessons for "A Circle of Sun" by Rebecca Kai Dotlich

PHONICS: WORD ENDINGS—(-*ING*)

Introduce the -*ing* ending. Draw attention to the ending by having individual students come up and circle a word from the poem that ends in -*ing*. List those finds on chart paper: *dancing*, *leaping*, *skipping*, *swinging*, and *singing*. Point out that *morning* doesn't fit in this lesson because the -*ing* is not an ending in this case. *Morning* is a noun that tells us the time of day. It is not an action verb, because *morn* isn't something we can do.

A CIRCLE OF SUN
by Rebecca Kai Dotlich

I'm dancing.

I'm leaping.

I'm skipping about.

I gallop.

I grin.

I giggle.

I shout.

I'm Earth's many colors.

I'm morning and night.

I'm honey on toast.

I'm funny.

I'm bright.

I'm swinging.

I'm singing.

I wiggle.

I run.

I'm a piece of the sky

in a circle of sun.

Source: *Here's a Little Poem: A Very First Book of Poetry* (Yolen & Peters, 2007)

Select one of the rules below. Focus on the words from the poem that follow the rule. Add several additional examples of your own to the list. Encourage students to be word detectives. As they read around the room or in their free reading time, ask them to look for other *-ing* words that follow this pattern. Then, return to teach the other rules at another time with a different teachable poem.

Rules:

If the word is CVVC or CVCC, just add *-ing* (*leaping, swinging, singing*)

If there is a silent *e*, drop the *e* and add *-ing* (*dance/dancing*)

If the word is CVC or CCVC, double the final consonant (*hop/hopping, grin/grinning, skip/skipping*)

MEANING VOCABULARY: ANTONYMS

Review the poem. Explain that you will be working with antonyms, or words that mean the opposite of each other. Model by writing down several examples of antonyms:

hot/cold   happy/sad   dirty/clean   tall/short

If you have one available, introduce a thesaurus that offers both synonyms and antonyms. Look up *hot* together and find another word that is an opposite other than *cold*. Divide students into learning triads, supply each group with a thesaurus, and work on *grin, giggle, shout, run*, and *funny*. Share the findings together, creating an antonym list for future reading and writing work.

WRITING

Guide students in noticing that "A Circle of Sun" is a list poem. Underline the action verbs and adjectives that help describe the child in the poem. During writing workshop, compose a list poem that answers the question "Who are you?" Work with students to brainstorm and record additional action words so that writers can use them as they create list poems about themselves. Help budding poets by giving them a framework initially. Once their confidence blossoms, they can write a list poem without this scaffolding. Remind poets that rhyming is NOT required.

I'm _____.

I'm _____.

I'm _____.

I _____.

I _____.

I _____.

I'm glad to be me!

Picture Book Pairings for "A Circle of Sun"

I Love My Hair! (Tarpley, 1998) As a mother combs and braids her daughter's hair, she relates her rich cultural heritage.

The Skin You Live In (Tyler, 2005) This is a poetic celebration of diversity.

Perfect Poetry for Many Voices: More Poems and Mini-Lessons

"Whooo?" by Lilian Moore (unpaged)

Found In: *Beware, Take Care: Fun and Spooky Poems* by Lilian Moore (Moore, 2006)

Summary of Poem: The interactions between the wind and an owl are a little spooky to a child.

Phonemic Awareness: Medial Sounds

Listen to the poem being read aloud. Reread it again, asking students to put their hand up whenever they hear the ooo and long e sounds. Ask volunteers to say another word that has these same sounds.

Phonics: Digraphs—/wh/

Teach students about the digraph /wh/. Explain that the w and the h sometimes team up to make one sound, as they do in the word *Wheee*, from Moore's poem. At other times, students will hear a /h/ sound like *who*. Put a list of selected words on the document camera, overhead transparency, or board. Read each one, emphasizing the beginning sounds. Have students repeat them: *whale, wheel, whistle, where, who, what, white, when, why,* and *which*.

Fluency

Read through the poem once. Next, have the children echo-read it with you to familiarize themselves with the words. Work in small groups, practicing the poem chorally. Follow up by dividing the class into three groups, one for the owl, one for the wind, and one for "me"—making it a poem for three voices. Read and enjoy. Switch voices for additional practice.

Picture Book Pairings

The Wind Blew (Hutchins, 1993). The wind's game causes many people to chase after their belongings.

The Littlest Owl (Pitcher, 2008). Last to be born, the littlest owl is determined to catch up with his siblings.

"Me x 2" by Jane Medina (p. 84)

Found In: *Days to Celebrate: A Full Year of Poetry, People, Holidays, History, Fascinating Facts, and More* (Hopkins, 2005)

Summary of Poem: Written in English and Spanish, this poem illustrates the challenges of speaking more than one language.

Meaning Vocabulary: Homophones

To help students with spelling and word meaning, teach them about the homophones in this poem. Teach the children that homophones are words that sound the same but are spelled differently and have different meanings. Write the words *two/to/*

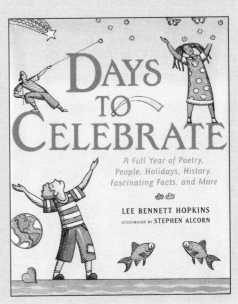

too, write/right, and *son/sun* on chart paper, document camera, or board. Ask the class to read each set of words with you. Check word knowledge by inviting volunteers to explain the meanings of the words in each set. Next, teach the students that they can use the context of what they are reading or writing to help them select the correct word when they are puzzled. Model several examples.

Right refers to being correct about something or to a specific direction.

I figured out the *right* answer.

I turned *right* when I left the classroom.

The word *write* is tied to a written message, like writing in class or communicating with someone else.

I like to *write* poetry.

We will *write* a thank-you note to the policeman who came to visit our class.

When other examples of homophones appear in read-alouds, teach a quick review lesson to keep this knowledge base growing.

Fluency

Medina's poem is an excellent choice to read aloud in two voices, one English and one echoed in Spanish. Invite a willing child from your class, another classroom, or a teacher who could take the part in Spanish. This would be an ideal selection to record and keep in the listening center for future enjoyment and Spanish language practice.

Comprehension: Thinking About Characters

This poem is written in first-person point of view from a child who speaks two languages. Discuss with children how they think the character feels about being bilingual. Continue this conversation during read-aloud time or guided reading with other stories about the experiences of bilingual children.

Picture Book Pairings

My Name Is Yoon (Recorvits, 2003). After moving from Korea, Yoon struggles to adjust to life in America.

A Day's Work (Bunting, 1994). A young boy helps his immigrant grandfather through a job-related misunderstanding.

Noisy Poems: More Poems and Mini-Lessons

"City Music" by Tony Mitton (p. 24)

Found In: *Poems Go Clang! A Collection of Noisy Verse* (Carsley et al., 1997)

Summary of Poem: The rhythms of busy city life fill this poem.

Phonics: Making Words

To practice segmenting words into their phonemes, linking sounds to letters, and blending vowel and consonant sounds, try a making-words activity. Children use the Making Words reproducible found in Appendix 2 on page 143. Make the words using large letter cards in a pocket chart following the sample lesson below.

This word is *tap*.   t-a-p

Point to and say each phoneme as you read the word. Then blend the sounds together slowly as you repeat the word. Continue in the same manner with the other words after children have given each word a try on their own.

[Next four lines are teacher's language.]

Let's change one letter and make *tip*.   t-i-p
Change another letter and make *sip*.   s-i-p
Now, change another letter and make *rip*.   r-i-p
Last, let's change one letter and make *rap*. r-a-p

Invite students to change one letter and make another new word to share with the class.

Options for Differentiation

Older students can begin with four-letter words such as *ding* or *snap*. With the latter, you might change letters to make such words as *snip*, *slip*, *flip*, and *flop*, and challenge students to try more than one change from *flop* to *stop*. Review the meanings of the words you create.

Fluency

Practice this poem over several days, making sure students understand the words and have mastered the rhythm. Talk together about what kinds of actions they could use as they reflect the city sounds. Find a collection of possible "instruments" around the classroom. These might include pencils to be tapped together or on desktops, a "rattle" consisting of a container filled with number cubes, a bicycle horn, and a wastebasket transformed into a drum. Divide the class into pairs or triads, depending on class size. Assign one line and action per group, but the whole class might join in on the last line. Practice several times with the instruments. A small group might enjoy perfecting this to performance quality.

Picture Book Pairings

Big City Song (Pearson, 2006). City sounds fill the air day and night.

Busy, Busy City Street (Meister, 2000). Rhyming text describes many noises in a bustling city.

"Manhattan Lullaby" by Norma Farber (p. 90)

Found In: *Here's a Little Poem: A Very First Book of Poetry* (Yolen & Peters, 2007)

Summary of Poem: While it might seem noisy to children from the country, city sounds lull city children to sleep.

Phonemic Awareness: Syllables

Read the poem aloud. Ask the children what's happening in this poem to check for understanding. Give them an example of a one-syllable word and a two-syllable word from the poem. Clap out the syllables for each word. Have the children do it with you. Now, ask them to listen for more two-syllable words as you read the poem again. Go through the poem two lines at a time, repeating a line if children need to hear the words again. They are to clap twice each time they hear a two-syllable word. Conclude by picking two or three interesting two-syllable words such as *rumble*, *wailing*, and *babble* to discuss with the listeners, talking about the way these words sound.

Phonics: Word Families—(-eep)

Make a list of all of the words in the poem that end in the *-eep* pattern. Tell children that they can chunk this word family ending when they are sounding out words. First, they sound out the onset, and then chunk the rime. Try this with /b/ . . . -*eep* and /sl/ . . . -*eep*. Play an "I'm Thinking of . . ." guessing game with the class to add more words to this word family:

> I'm thinking of an animal that gives us wool. (*sheep*)
>
> I'm thinking of a kind of vehicle that's good on rough roads. (*jeep*)
>
> I'm thinking of a sound that a bird makes. (*cheep*)

Children might come up with their own *-eep* riddles as you add more words to this family over the next few days.

Comprehension: Conversing and Connecting

Do a compare and contrast activity with "City Music" (see p. 71). As with all of the poems, be certain children can retell you what is happening in the poem as a comprehension check. Rereading poetry does help improve fluency, but fluency without comprehension is valuable time and effort wasted. Use the familiar Venn diagram to compare and contrast the two poems. Wrap up the examination by writing several sentences about life in the city based upon what the poems highlight and what children have actually experienced.

Picture Book Pairings

Clang! Clang! Beep! Beep! Listen to the City (Burleigh, 2009). Listen to the varied sounds throughout the day in a busy city.

Street Music: City Poems (Adoff, 1995). Experience the sights and sounds of the city through a collection of 15 poems.

POETIC PICTURE BOOKS AND ANTHOLOGIES PERFECT FOR PERFORMING	
Title	**Brief Summary**
Cinder-Elly (Minters, 1994)	This is an upbeat version of Cinderella.
City I Love (Hopkins, 2009)	Many aspects of busy city life are highlighted in different poems.
If You're Happy and You Know It: Jungle Edition (Warhola, 2007)	Jungle animals sing this song with related movements and sounds.
Let Me Be the Boss: Poems for Kids to Perform (Bagert, 1992)	Enjoy this selection of funny poems for your students to perform in your classroom.
The Little Blue Truck (Schertle, 2008)	Children will enjoy how these friends help each other in time of trouble.
Messing Around on the Monkey Bars and Other School Poems for Two Voices (Franco, 2009)	A collection of school poems for two voices. It ends with suggestions of adventurous ways to read the poems.
Mice Squeak, We Speak (Shapiro, 1997)	Simple rhyming text, coupled with Tomie dePaola's illustrations, describe the different ways animals communicate.
More Pocket Poems (Katz, 2009)	Kids will enjoy this brightly illustrated collection of short poems that are perfect for performing.
Whoever You Are (Fox, 1997)	This book ties children from varying cultures together through similarities and differences.
You Read to Me, I'll Read to You: Very Short Scary Tales to Read Together (Hoberman, 2007)	This is the fourth book in this popular series of simple rhyming, illustrated stories for two voices. Kids who love scary tales will enjoy this one!

MEANINGFUL FLUENCY DEVELOPMENT ACTIVITIES

Translating Research Into Sensible Daily Practice

In many of today's schools, measures of a child's reading speed and accuracy are being used as one indicator of his or her reading achievement. A great deal of attention is given to the number of words a child can read in one minute and whether this rate is improving over time. While this may be considered helpful data for screening students, it does not take into account other important aspects of fluency, such as phrasing and prosody, or reading with expression (Allington, 2009). To boost reading fluency, all readers, and especially our struggling students, need to develop the following:

- Useful decoding skills and strategies
- Robust meaning vocabularies
- Strong sight vocabularies
- The ability to self-monitor as they read
- Flexible and effective comprehension strategies
- Intrinsic motivation to read purposely and voluntarily (Allington, 2009)

One of the simplest and most effective practices you can incorporate into your daily routine is to model fluent reading. Every time you read a poem aloud to students or share a related picture book, you are demonstrating how reading should sound. That's fluency instruction!

Another research-approved method is having children engage in repeated readings of a poem or book. Pearson and Fielding (1996) reported that repeated oral reading increased comprehension in poor readers based upon the combination of seeing and hearing the words, that the dual input helped them better understand the text. Think about incorporating the following rereading options into your daily core reading instruction.

USING POETRY TO STRENGTHEN STUDENTS' READING FLUENCY	
Rereading Options	**Explanation**
Whole-Group Choral Reading	Read poems chorally, letting your voices blend into one. This approach is a must for ELLs, who can practice words and language in a non-threatening manner. Choral reading helps develop oral language skills and also builds fluency along the way (Hadaway, Vardell, & Young, 2001).
Shared Reading	Another way to savor poetry together is through shared reading (Fountas & Pinnell, 1996; Reutzel & Cooter, 2008). Along with the enjoyment shared reading provides, you are improving word recognition, reading rate, and expressive reading, all at the same time (Ming & Dukes, 2008; Rasinski, 2006). LaDonna Wicklund (1989) adapted this approach and found that it was tremendously successful in motivating and improving the skills of her struggling readers. Wicklund used the following process: • Choose a poem that matches the interests and experiences of the students. • Enlarge the poem for easy viewing. • Read it aloud while pointing to the words. • Reread it several times, taking turns pointing to particular words, reading with expression, or looking for familiar words. • Invite students to illustrate personal copies of the poem. • Work with individual lines, cutting the line into words and unscrambling them. • Cut the poem into lines and have students sequence it. • Teach selected vocabulary words or review sight words. • Tie in writing. You might start with a poem patterned after the one you are working on. • Dramatize the poem.
Reading Around the Circle	Once children are familiar with a poem, have them sit in several small circles. Select a student to begin. Children in each circle read a line, followed by the child on their right (or left), until the poem is complete.
Reading in a Round	Pick a simple, rhythmic poem. Divide the class in half. One half of the class begins by reading the first line of the poem. At that point, the other half begins reading the poem, proceeding as you would when singing a round such as the song "Row, Row, Row Your Boat."
Popcorn-Style Reading	Much like this sounds, one child at a time pops up to read a line in the poem. You might assign numbers to the lines in the poem, let children select a number, and then read the poem number by number to avoid the confusion of several children popping up at the same time (Vardell, 2009).
Tag-Team Partner Reading	Partners take turns reading a poem line-by-line, or a book page-by-page. Partner one reads a line or page, and then partner two reads the next line or page, and so on until the end. If you are looking for a collection of poems for partner reading, try *Partner Poems for Building Fluency* by Bobbi Katz (1996).
Solo Silent Reading	Children read poetry quietly during independent reading.

Reading Into a Tape Recorder or iPod	Children love to hear themselves read. Set up a listening center where learners can practice reading a poem. To begin, have students record themselves reading the poem aloud. Then, ask them to listen to the recording and critique their fluency. After a few days of repeated reading, children record the poem again and celebrate their improvements.
Cloze Reading	Display a poem but put in a blank line for every four or five words, depending on the poem. Read the poem aloud, pausing for children to fill in the blanks.
Listening Center	Give students time to listen to the sounds of poetry by placing an enticing selection of poems in your listening center and refreshing the poems on a regular basis.

CHAPTER 5

IMAGINE! POEMS TO TAKE YOU AWAY

"I Know a Way to Open Doors" by Karla Kuskin

I know a way to open doors

and find adventure, tears and pleasure

where witches whisper,

frogs are men

and pirates on wild shores

call us to join a quest for untold treasure.

There

what we find depends on where we look.

A thousand worlds, or more, await us.

Travel with me,

come,

we'll go by the book.

Source: *Moon, Have You Met My Mother? The Collected Poems of Karla Kuskin*
(Kuskin, 2003)

Open Doors to Imagination

One of the invaluable gifts we can give our students is time to strengthen their imaginations. The worlds of handheld technology and vivid, action-driven movies fill many a child's mind with images. Few of those images, however, stimulate creative and fanciful thinking in the way that good books and cleverly crafted poems do. The poems in this chapter are irresistible tickets to untraveled places, both real and imaginary. If we are lucky, they may be the ticket that opens a reluctant reader's heart and mind to the world of books.

What might it be like to be a geographer or an astronaut? To sail the skies on the back of a dragon? To surf the high seas and battle fearsome pirates? Lead the way by inviting your students to journey far and wide through the books and poetry that you bring them each day.

Mini-Lessons for "I Know a Way to Open Doors" by Karla Kuskin

TEACHING IDEA

To create excitement for poetry, place Kuskin's poem in the middle of a bulletin board. Then gather a collection of your favorite poems for students to read and review. Once they've each found a poem they love, invite them to write the title, draw a picture of the poem, and recommend it to a friend. Post the students' poetry suggestions on the bulletin board. When they have time to read around the room, encourage learners to make a stop here, selecting a poem or two from a nearby binder containing copies of the recommended poems.

PHONICS: MAKING WORDS—TREASURE

Draw attention to the spelling of words by playing a word game. Without telling the students which word you are using, hand out the Making Words (Cunningham & Cunningham, 1992) reproducible on page 143 in the appendix. While you are playing with letters and words, you are also building listening skills. Working with scrambled letters from the word *treasure*, follow these steps:

> Find three letters that make the word *rat*.
>
> Change one letter to make *sat*
>
> Find three letters to make the word *tea*.
>
> Now change one letter to make *sea*.
>
> Find four letters to make the word *rest*.
>
> Continue in the same manner, making the words *star, tear, sure, steer,* and *stare.*

At this point, issue the challenge, "Take all eight letters and make the mystery word." Once children have had a chance to try it on their own, ask whether they would like a "letter clue" or a "meaning clue" to help them figure out the word. An example of a letter clue is "The word begins with the letter *t*." A meaning clue would be "Pirates are always looking for this." Making Words is a multilevel activity that helps struggling readers strengthen letter-sound relationships and learn how to look for patterns in words.

FLUENCY

As you read the poem orally, model the phrasing you would use so the poem makes sense. On a displayed copy, mark where you plan to pause as you read aloud. Then, demonstrate for students how pausing at these spots increases understanding. So that children can hear as well as experience the value of proper phrasing, read through the poem in an echo format. Practice one more time by rereading it chorally. Return to the poem the following day and practice the phrasing once more. Add the poem to poetry binders for future fluency practice and enjoyment.

> ### Picture Book Pairings for "I Know a Way to Open Doors"
>
> --------
>
> *Miss Smith's Incredible Storybook* (Garland, 2003)
> When Miss Smith reads to her class, storybook characters come to life.
>
> *Read All About It!* (Bush & Bush, 2008)
> Tyrone thinks reading is boring until the stories begin to come alive.

Mini-Lessons for "When I'm an Astronaut" by Bobbi Katz

SIGHT VOCABULARY

This poem presents an excellent opportunity to review a number of sight words. Select the sight words you would like learners to practice. For example, you might write the words *first, get, my, then, to, the, right, when,* and *all* on large index cards. Read through an enlarged copy of the poem. Next, hold one sight word up, ask a volunteer to read it and then come up to draw a box around it in the poem. For a little more practice, chorally reread the poem, asking the students to emphasize the boxed words as they read them.

MEANING VOCABULARY: COMPOUND WORDS

After reading and discussing the poem, write the three compound words, *spacesuit, spacecraft,* and *countdown,* on sentence strips, and then cut each word into its two parts. Place the two words in a pocket chart close together, forming the compound word. Read the words. Ask the students what makes these words unique. If no one detects that each word is made from two individual words to create a new word, point that out. Separate the words in the pocket chart, read the single words, and then put them together again. Explain how readers can usually figure out the meaning of

WHEN I'M AN ASTRONAUT
by Bobbi Katz

First I'll get into my spacesuit.

Then I'll bravely wave good-by.

Next I'll climb into my spacecraft

Built to sail right through the sky!

In command inside the capsule,

I will talk to ground control.

When we've checked out

   all the systems,

I'll say, "Let the countdown roll!"

And it's 4-3-2-1—blast off—

With a smile upon my face,

I'll spin loops around the planets

up, up, up in outer space!

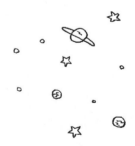

Source: *Blast Off! Poems About Space* (Hopkins, 1995)

compound words by breaking the words apart, thinking about the meaning of the pieces, and then reassembling the word. For additional practice, have students work with partners. Give each pair a compound word and two index cards. One child writes the first part of the compound word on an index card while his or her partner writes the second part of the word on a separate card. Then, each partner illustrates his or her word part on the back of the card. Share with the class. Compound words that are easily illustrated include *bookworm, cupcake, hotdog, birdbath, toothbrush, sailboat,* and *doghouse.*

WRITING

Point out that the astronaut in this poem worked through a series of steps before taking off. Read the poem together and ask the students to figure out what she did first, next, and last. Write the three transition words, *first, next,* and *then,* for easy viewing. Model how to use transition words as you write about how you got ready for school that morning. Put students into writing duos or triads to write about a familiar procedure. Share. Remind students of how helpful transition words can be in their future writing.

Options for Differentiation

Working with the classroom assistant or another student in the room, explain to your ELLs or to the whole class that some of the words in this poem have several different meanings—for example, *wave, sail, command,* and *ground.* Check background knowledge by asking children to define these words. Tell them that you are looking for at least two meanings for each word. Once reviewed, students can gather these words in their own picture dictionary that illustrates different word meanings. This will be a handy resource when reading and writing.

Picture Book Pairings for "When I'm an Astronaut"

If You Decide to Go to the Moon (McNulty, 2005)
Join a boy on his imaginary trip to the moon.

Roaring Rockets: Amazing Machines (Mitton, 2000)
In this nonfiction book, three silly animals blast off into space.

A Poem to Pair With "When I'm an Astronaut"

"Rickety Train Ride" by Tony Mitton (pp. 78–79)

Found In: *Here's a Little Poem: A Very First Book of Poetry* (Yolen & Peters, 2007)

Summary of Poem: A child describes his trip on an imaginary train.

Phonics: Consonant Blends—/cl/ and /tr/

After enjoying the poem together, work with the /cl/ and /tr/ blends in the first verse. Display the words *clickety*, *clack*, *trickety*, and *track*. Read each word, emphasizing the beginning blends. Explain that two consonants work together to form a beginning blend and that blends appear in many words that students will read and write. Ask children to confer with partners to think of other words they know or can find around the room beginning with /cl/ and /tr/. Add suggestions to a list and post it for later reference as students do their own writing.

Fluency

Read the poem aloud to students as they follow along on their own copies. Then, echo-read it. Ask students to listen to the rhythm of the poem, pointing out that it sounds a little like the wheels of a train. Next, give each child a pair of rhythm sticks. Read the poem chorally, clicking out the rhythm. To master the words and improve fluency, students can practice reading the poem in pairs.

Writing

Using a copy of the poem that all children can see, ask volunteers to come up and circle the nonsense words *trickety*, *thickety*, and *drippety*. Read the words together. Discuss how poets often play with words to make a poem silly or fun to read. Write some familiar words on a chart and invite students to work together to add the *-ety* ending to create smile-inducing words. Suggestions could include *slick*, *bounce*, and *thump*.

Options for Differentiation

Be certain that your ELLs understand the difference between the real words and the nonsense words that occur in the poem. Show visuals of the real words to enhance understanding. Invite learners to use the words in sentences to be certain they understand the meaning of each word.

Picture Book Pairings

Seymour Simon's Book of Trains (Simon, 2004). Train enthusiasts will learn about different kinds of trains and how they work.

Trainstop (Lehman, 2008). In this wordless picture book, a young girl takes a fanciful train ride.

JUNIOR GEOGRAPHER
by Maria Walther and Katherine Phillips

(Sung to the tune of "Yankee Doodle")

I'm a junior geographer
I study the earth and land.
And when I don't know where to go,
A map gives me a hand.

Deserts, mountains, seas, and lakes
People and locations.
We will learn about the world,
Then take some great vacations.

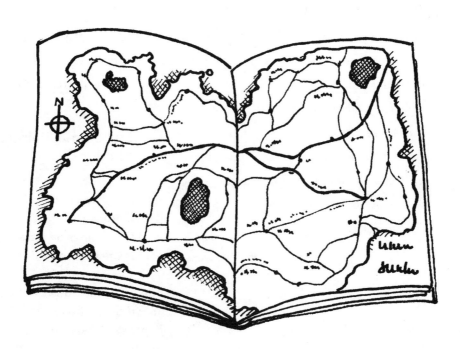

Mini-Lessons for "Junior Geographer" by Maria Walther and Katherine Phillips

FLUENCY

Read the poem chorally. Then, reread it, working on rhythm and expression. Model how some poems can be set to music, singing this poem to the tune of "Yankee Doodle." As with other poems throughout the book, groups can continue to practice, polishing rhythm and expression before signing up to present it during a Poetry Break

MEANING VOCABULARY: GEOGRAPHY WORDS

Ask your learners what they already know about the geography words, *mountains, lakes, deserts,* and *seas.* If needed, teach them the terms using child-friendly explanations and illustrations from nonfiction texts. Then, have student pairs use the Word Concept Chart on page 146 of the appendix to extend their understanding of these geographical terms. Model the process using the word *earth,* inviting student contributions to complete the map. Discuss the fact that each pair of students will come up with different characteristics and examples, so each Word Concept Chart will be a unique look at a word. Assign a word to each pair, and monitor student work. Use a document camera, overhead transparencies, or bulletin board to share completed maps with the poem for additional study.

MEANING VOCABULARY TO HIGHLIGHT FOR ELLS

Gather a collection of nonfiction books or bookmark a few Internet sites that display geographical features. A helpful set of nonfiction books is Lerner's First Step Nonfiction Landforms series including, among other titles, *Islands* and *Mountains* (Anderson, 2008). During guided reading, work with your English language learners to make vocabulary cards of the geographical words accompanied by a picture. Review the words with these learners, showing them where to find more information on each word if they are interested. Students might want to locate these features on a map of their home country and tell the class a bit about a particular feature.

> ### Picture Book Pairings for "Junior Geographer"
> -----------------------
>
> *Adèle & Simon in America* (McClintock, 2008)
> Join the siblings on a train trip across the United States.
>
> *The Scrambled States of America Talent Show* (Keller, 2008)
> Kansas is tired of being in the same location and convinces the other states to change places.

A BOOK
by Myra Cohn Livingston

Closed, I am a mystery.

Open, I will always be

a friend with whom you think and see.

Closed, there's nothing I can say.

Open, we can dream and stray

to other worlds, far and away.

Source: *School Supplies: A Book of Poems* (Hopkins, 1996)

Mini-Lessons for "A Book" by Myra Cohn Livingston

PHONICS: WORD FAMILIES— (-AY)

Focusing on word families will be a valuable review for some of your learners and a direct teaching lesson for struggling readers. Write *-ay* on a chart for easy viewing. Teach the students that chunking words into their onset and rime will help them figure out new words. Write the words *say*, *stray*, and *clay* on the chart. Ask students to repeat them after you. Break the words into onsets and rimes, /s/ + *-ay* = *say*, /str/ + *-ay* = *stray*, and /cl/ + *-ay* = *clay*, highlighting the fact that they all belong to the *-ay* family. Brainstorm more words to add to this extensive family. Post the list for easy reference.

COMPREHENSION: ELEMENTS OF A MYSTERY

Read "A Book" aloud to the class. Point out that this poem presents a bit of a mystery to be solved, and readers will need to look for clues to solve that mystery. In the process, they are inferring and predicting, two critical comprehension strategies. Model how you would use these elements to solve a mini-mystery in this poem or in a read-aloud using the Elements of a Mystery chart below.

Elements of a Mystery

A Puzzling Happening: I wonder what the object is?

The Detective: Me

The Clues: It can open and close. Hmmm. I'm going to predict that it's a door. Let me read to see if I'm right.

Now that I've reread the poem, a door doesn't make sense.

When it's open, it's a friend that helps me see something and think about something. I don't think that's a door. I'm going to revise my thinking. I guess that it's . . .

The Solution: I know! It's a book!

To continue practicing these strategies, give brief book talks on popular mystery series books, including Jigsaw Jones, Cam Jansen, or Nate the Great. Struggling readers quickly recognize the characters in series books and benefit from a familiar format. They can move on to the next book without having to spend time getting to know new characters or another author's writing style. The more they read, the better they get!

MEANING VOCABULARY: ANTONYMS

After reading and guessing what object the poem is describing, teach a review lesson on antonyms. Using the words *open* and *closed* from this poem, follow the format for the lesson on page 68 (Chapter 4, "A Circle of Sun," mini-lesson on Meaning Vocabulary: Antonyms). Add three more examples of commonly occurring antonyms, such as *high/low, near/far,* and *fast/slow* to your ongoing list for the students to use.

Mini-Lessons for "Cat Kisses" by Bobbi Katz

PHONICS: DIGRAPHS—/CH/

Focus on consonant digraphs for a quick lesson on the /ch/ sound. Teach the students that the two letters work together to make a new sound that is different from the individual letter sounds. Write the words *cheek* and *chin* on an overhead, document camera, or board. Read these aloud, separating them into onset and rimes. Add three familiar nouns from the Dolch nouns list—*chair, chicken,* and *children,* for example— reading them the same way, with the students repeating each one. Review these and other examples by tucking them into the morning message or highlighting them as you read aloud. Dolch word lists and a variety of activities are easily accessed online.

COMPREHENSION: MENTAL IMAGES

Without showing the title, read the poem to your students. Then, ask them to draw what they imagine or can infer from the clues in the poem. Share and discuss the images and the thinking behind them. Remind readers that using clues to create images or to infer helps them to better understand a writer's ideas. Now, reread the poem, pinpointing the clues that children used.

Picture Book Pairings for "Cat Kisses"

Wabi Sabi (Reibstein, 2008)
A little cat in Kyoto, Japan, learns the meaning of her name.

The Chocolate Cat (Stainton, 2007)
A chocolate maker and his clever cat change life in their quiet town.

CAT KISSES

by Bobbi Katz

Sandpaper kisses
On a cheek or a chin
That is the way
For a day to begin!

Sandpaper kisses
A cuddle, a purr.
I have an alarm clock
Covered with fur.

Here's a Little Poem: A Very First Book of Poetry (Yolen & Peters, 2007)

A Poem to Pair With "Cat Kisses"

"The Toaster" by William Jay Smith (p. 35)

Found In: *Read-Aloud Rhymes for the Very Young* (Prelutsky, 1986)

Summary of Poem: An imaginative child pretends that his toaster is a dragon.

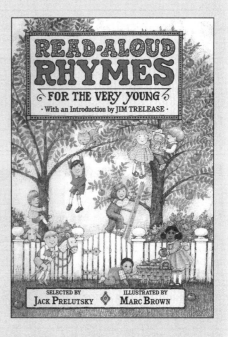

Fluency

A group of four students might like to read this for the class, one line per student, adding expression and working on pacing. Other students can practice this in pairs or take a copy home in their poetry binders to read with a family member. Remind readers to adjust their rate as they read until they master all of the words and can read the poem smoothly.

Meaning Vocabulary: Homophones

To help students with spelling and word meanings, teach them about the homophones in this poem. Write the words *red/read, one/won, by/bye* and *sees/seas* where everyone can see them. Then, follow the lesson plan on page 69.

Writing

Discuss how the poet used descriptive words and imagination to make an everyday object like a toaster into a fire-breathing, toast-making dragon. Underline the descriptive words in the first two lines. Then, have students think about the way the toaster is brought to life. Model, using descriptive words to add personality to the classroom pencil sharpener, a trashcan, or other familiar objects. Once you have selected an item, brainstorm descriptive words so that students have a helpful resource when writing. After working together on this example, put students in small groups, each working with a different item. Bring familiar items from home to add to classroom objects. Each group will begin by brainstorming descriptive words. Monitor progress. Share results as a whole class and display on a creative writing bulletin board.

Picture Book Pairings

The Best Pet of All (LaRochelle, 2004). A young boy asks a dragon to help convince his mother that he should have a dog.

The Egg (Robertson, 2001). When George hatches an unusual egg, he finds an unusual pet—a dragon.

POETIC PICTURE BOOKS AND ANTHOLOGIES TO STIR THE IMAGINATION	
Title	**Brief Summary**
Barn Dance (Martin & Archambault, 1986)	On a sleepless night a boy follows the sounds of revelry to the barn.
Behold the Bold Umbrellaphant: And Other Poems (Prelutsky, 2006)	Imaginative poems combine parts of real animals with inanimate objects, with grin-inducing results.
Felicity Floo Visits the Zoo (Redmond, 2009)	A sniffly girl and some sneezing animals will have your students looking for tissues.
Flotsam (Weisner, 2006)	A child finds an ancient underwater camera filled with imagination-stretching photos.
Henry's Amazing Imagination! (Carlson, 2008)	Henry's teacher encourages him to write down his imaginary tales.
My Dinosaur (Weatherby, 1997)	A young girl sails across the skies on her dinosaur.
My Special Day at Third Street School (Bunting, 2009)	This rhyming book tells of a class's preparation for a visiting author.
Vroomaloom Zoom (Coy, 2000)	Coy's rhythmic, repetitive text makes this book about an imaginary car trip a joy to read aloud.
Wild About Books (Sierra, 2004)	When the bookmobile goes to the zoo, all of the animals get into the reading and writing spirit.
Yellow Elephant: A Bright Bestiary (Larios, 2006)	Ordinary animals come in fresh colors in these short poems.

Thoughtful Comprehension Lessons

Translating Research Into Sensible Daily Practice

Reading is a meaning-making process. Whether students are reading poetry, stories, or nonfiction books, their understanding of the text is key. Certainly, we strive to ensure that all of our readers are making meaning as they read. Sadly, despite our efforts, some students will still experience difficulties. The act of comprehending is a complex process; therefore, it is often difficult to determine the factor or factors that are standing in the way of our struggling readers' success. As you work with your learners, consider the following possible impediments to comprehension. Does the student

- lack background knowledge and experiences to connect with and understand the information in the text?
- require instruction in the word-recognition skills that are needed to decode automatically?
- read word-by-word, resulting in poor fluency?
- have underdeveloped oral language capabilities?
- need a stronger foundation in meaning vocabulary?
- read texts that are simply too difficult?

Think about the impact of just the last factor. Difficult text causes children to get bogged down trying to decode words. That, in turn, slows their fluency and impedes understanding. We have consciously included lessons in this book that address each of these roadblocks to comprehension. Along with tackling the underlying causes of poor comprehension, we know it is important to help readers build a repertoire of strategies. See chart on page 92 for a list of essential comprehension strategies and skills.

There is a wealth of research supporting the idea that we can boost our students' comprehension if we explicitly teach *even one* of the strategies for comprehending text (National Reading Panel, 2000; Pearson, Roehler, Dole, & Duffy, 1992; Pressley, 2000). Furthermore, if we model and teach readers how to use multiple strategies at once, the results are even more powerful (Duke & Pearson, 2002). For example, prior to sharing a poem, you might read the title to the students and ask them to activate their background knowledge and predict what they think the poem might be about. Then, while you are reading aloud, pause and remind children to self-monitor and check for understanding as you go, stopping now and then to discuss important ideas. After reading, ask students to summarize or ask any questions they have about the poem. Adding this simple yet effective routine to your powerful reading instruction will help your learners soar.

USING POETRY TO STRENGTHEN COMPREHENSION STRATEGIES AND SKILLS	
Self-Monitoring/ Clarifying	Show students how you pause while reading a poem to consider the meaning or reflect on your understanding. Make your classroom a place where thinking is visible, and celebrate children's efforts to revise and clarify their thinking as they work to understand a poem.
Activating Background Knowledge and Predicting	Prior to reading a poem, discuss what students already know about the topic. Teach children strategies for building background knowledge. For example, before reading the poem "Junior Geographer" found on page 83, you could send readers on an Internet search to discover what a geographer does. It's also important to show students how to use context clues to help predict unknown words.
Inferring	Model how readers use the information from the text along with their background knowledge to draw conclusions and formulate novel interpretations of a poem. Inferring plays a critical role in poetry reading because poets don't use as many words or write as literally as the authors of most other texts, so the reader has to "fill in the blanks."
Questioning	Demonstrate how readers ask questions before, during, and after reading. Be certain to model different types of questions, such as questions to clarify the meaning of the poem or a word in the poem, questions about the author's poetic style, or ponderings inspired by the content of the poem.
Visualizing	Encourage children to visualize or make mental images as you read poems aloud. The use of sensory language makes poems ideal for demonstrating and guiding students as they practice visualization. Using these images helps readers draw conclusions, create unique interpretations of the text, and remember important details. In addition, incorporating images from reading enhances students' writing (Miller, 2002).
Determining Important Information	*What is the big idea in this poem?* Questions such as this one will help readers zero in on the key ideas or the theme of a poem. Allow for a little wiggle room here as not everyone will have the same ideas.
Thinking About Text Structure	Poets employ unique text structures, use conventions in creative ways, play with language, and adjust phrasing. Together, these elements play a role in understanding and interpreting the meaning of the words. Capitalize on opportunities to show readers how the elements of poetry work together to create a unique kind of text structure.
Summarizing	This challenging task is more than retelling. Model the process several times before students try it on their own. Teach them to find the main idea or ideas in the poem. Less important details are not included. To summarize, write a topic sentence and add just a few more sentences that explain *mainly* what the poem is about (Duke & Pearson, 2002).
Synthesizing	To help learners synthesize the poetry selections that you share, provide opportunities for them to respond to the text in various ways, such as through writing, art, and drama. In addition, make time for students to recommend poems to others and critique the poems they read.

CHAPTER 6

INVESTIGATE! POEMS TO ENHANCE SCIENCE INSTRUCTION

Read to Learn

With the increased emphasis on literacy instruction in many schools, the time devoted to science investigations is waning. Therefore, the more we can integrate science content into our literacy instruction, and vice versa, the better prepared students will be to read and understand nonfiction texts. This understanding is essential for our struggling readers as they transition from decoding words to more effortless reading—a shift that is sometimes characterized as moving from

learning to read toward *reading to learn*. Wise teachers, like you, use carefully selected poems as a vehicle to broaden students' knowledge of content area vocabulary and concepts. In addition, inviting children to write science-related poetry is a novel way to solidify learners' understanding of a topic or unit of study. To guide our selection of poetry in this chapter, we collected poems that represent two of the "big ideas" identified by the report *National Science Education Standards* (NRC, 1996). The first grouping of poems and mini-lessons illuminate the "big idea" of life science, including topics such as bugs, worms, frogs, and toads. The second section of the chapter contains appealing earth science poetry and accompanying teaching ideas.

CATERPILLARS
by Aileen L. Fisher

What do caterpillars do?
Nothing much but chew and chew.

What do caterpillars know?
Nothing much but how to grow.

They just eat what by and by
Will make them be a butterfly,

But that is more than I can do
However much I chew and chew.

Source: *The Bill Martin Jr. Big Book of Poetry* (Martin, 2009)

Mini-Lessons for "Caterpillars" by Aileen L. Fisher

PHONEMIC AWARENESS: BEGINNING BLEND SUBSTITUTION

Once you have read and enjoyed "Caterpillars" in a read-aloud
or shared reading format, select a word or two from the poem to
use as you play a quick beginning-blend substitution game. The
fast-paced game sounds something like this: "Say *grow*." [Students
say *grow*.] "Take off *gr-*, add *bl-*, and the word you hear is _____
[blow]." "Say *blow*." [Students say *blow*]. "Take off *bl-*, add *sl-*,
and the word you hear is _____ [slow]." Continue with the following words: *glow*, *snow*, and *crow*. Another word from the poem
that has numerous beginning blend substitutions is *by*, which you
can change to *try*, *sky*, *fly*, *sly*, and *cry*.

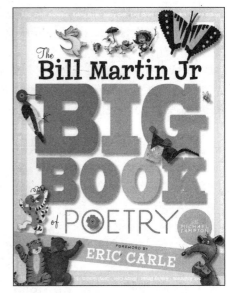

PHONICS: WORD SORT—/OW/ VS. /EW/

Contrast the words *know* and *grow* with the word *grew*—all found
in the poem. To explore the difference between words with the *-ow* pattern and the *-ew* pattern, students
can complete the word sort below. A reproducible version is provided in the appendix on page 141.

knew	grow	chew	know
slow	show	blew	low
tow	snow	few	new
threw	flew	glow	brew

For word sorting tips, see page 33.

COMPREHENSION: NONFICTION TEXT STRUCTURES—QUESTION AND ANSWER

The first two couplets of "Caterpillars" represent one of the text structures found in nonfiction writing—
the question and answer format. To explore the question and answer structure with your students, pair this
poem with the nonfiction picture book *What Do You Do With a Tail Like This?* (Jenkins & Page, 2003).
Help students see that the word *what*, found in both texts, signals the reader that a question is coming. In
a shared writing format, work together to compose a question and answer poem about another familiar
creature. Below we've included a sample about butterflies.

What do butterflies do?
They fly around, that's what they do.
What do butterflies eat?

They sip sweet nectar, that's what they eat.

Where do butterflies live?

They live all over, that's where they live.

How do butterflies grow?

They grow in stages, that's how they grow.

If you are interested in exploring other nonfiction text structures with your students, our book *Literature Is Back!* has a more detailed lesson plan that includes mentor texts and graphic organizers.

Bugs: More Poems and Mini-Lessons

"Caterpillar" by Valerie Worth (p. 60)

Found In: *All the Small Poems and Fourteen More* (Worth, 1994)

Summary of Poem: Follow the feet of a caterpillar down a twig to find his dinner.

Phonemic Awareness: Syllables
See the mini-lesson description on page 48 (Phonemic Awareness: Syllables)

one-syllable words: *feet, paws*
two-syllable words: *clever, patter*
three-syllable words: *another, caravan*
four-syllable word: *caterpillar*

Fluency
You'll notice that if you read each line of this poem separately, it doesn't make as much sense as when you combine certain lines into longer phrases. Work with your readers to decide where the pauses should go in order for this poem to make sense. On a displayed poem, mark each pause with a slash. Then, chorally reread "Caterpillar" using the predetermined breaks.

Writing
Valerie Worth uses sensory language and similes to portray a caterpillar's journey down a twig. Reread this poem from a writer's perspective to notice how she employs these craft techniques. Invite young writers to incorporate them into their own pieces during writing workshop.

Picture Book Pairings

Houdini the Amazing Caterpillar (Pedersen, 2008). Readers learn about the life cycle of a butterfly from Houdini, who amazes the students with his many "performances."

Where Butterflies Grow (Ryder, 1989). What does it feel like to change from a caterpillar into a butterfly? Read this book to find out.

"I Like Bugs" by Margaret Wise Brown

Found In: *I Like Bugs* (Brown, 1999)

Summary of Poem: The poet shares her enjoyment of bugs of all shapes and sizes.

Fluency

Once students are familiar with this poem, assign each child a line and read it popcorn style. See explanation on page 75.

Writing

Read and enjoy "I Like Bugs" either in the book or displayed on sentence strips in a pocket chart. Brainstorm and record a list of different kinds of bugs and another list of adjectives to describe bugs. Using Brown's pattern and the recorded words, students can create their own poem about their favorite bugs. See first-grader Levi's poem below.

I like _____ _____ _____ _____ _____ Any kind of _____ I like _____.	I like bugs Chocolate dung beetles Reddish fire ants Golden bees Shiny ladybugs Beautiful butterflies Any kind of bugs I like bugs. Written by: Levi

Picture Book Pairings

Insects Are My Life (McDonald, 1995). Amanda Frankenstein loves bugs of all kinds and sizes.

Velma Gratch & the Way Cool Butterfly (Madison, 2007). In trying to find an interest that will get her noticed, Velma discovers butterflies.

HEADS OR TAILS

by Lori Vicker

I found a wiggly worm,

He slithered very slow.

I picked him up so gently,

Then I tried to say "Hello."

But I was a bit confused,

As I held my little friend,

Was I speaking to his head,

Or was it his back end?

Source: *Poetry Parade* (Vicker, 2006)

Mini-Lessons for "Heads or Tails" by Lori Vicker

PHONICS: WORD ENDINGS—(-*ED*)

"Heads or Tails" has a few words with -*ed* endings, such as *slithered* and *picked*. To familiarize students with past tense verbs and -*ed* endings, play the following word game:

Today I pick, yesterday I _____ [picked].

Today I talk, yesterday I _____ [talked].

Today I play, yesterday I _____ [played].

Today I jump, yesterday I _____ [jumped].

Once students get the hang of this orally, give each child a small dry erase board and marker to play again. This time listeners will write the past-tense words on their boards.

COMPREHENSION: POINT OF VIEW

To boost comprehension, guide readers as they begin to understand that texts are written from different points of view. For example, point out that "Heads or Tails" is written from a person's viewpoint. Then, read aloud *Diary of a Worm* (Cronin, 2003), written from the worm's point of view. Compare and discuss the two texts. Another book to share, written from *two different* perspectives, is *Hey, Little Ant* (Hoose & Hoose, 1998).

MEANING VOCABULARY: ACTION VERBS

The worms in this poem *slither* and *wiggle*. Explore the different ways that animals move by reading *Move!* by Steve Jenkins and Robin Page (2006). Then make a chart of the various ways that animals get around. This will be a great resource for future writing projects.

Picture Book Pairings for "Heads or Tails"

- - - - - - - - - - - - - - - - - -

Chicken Cheeks (Black, 2009)
Enjoy this humorous picture book while learning different names for animals' rear ends.

Wiggle and Waggle (Arnold, 2007)
This easy-to-read beginning chapter book is about the adventures of two earthworms.

"Dirty Socks" by Bruce Lansky (pp. 72–73)

Found In: *Rolling in the Aisles: A Collection of Laugh-Out-Loud Poems* (Lansky, 2004)

Summary of Poem: After polluting a lake with his dirty socks, a child decides to bury them—watch out, worms!

Phonemic Awareness: Listening for Rhymes

After a few repeated readings, tell listeners that you are going to read the poem again, leaving out certain words, and that their job is to say the missing word. Then, reread the poem leaving out the second rhyming word in each stanza. Pause to let students chime in with the rhyming word.

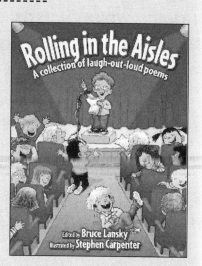

Phonics: Making Words—Pollution

See explanation of Making Words on page 71 and the reproducible of Making Words on pages 143–144 of the appendix. Working with scrambled letters from the word *pollution*, follow these steps:

- Find three letters that make the word *lot*.
- Change one letter to make the word *pot*.
- Repeat the same directions with: *tin/pin, not/nut*
- Find four letters that make the word *pool*.
- Change one letter to make the word *tool*.
- Find six letters that make the word *lotion*.
- Change one letter to make the word *potion*.
- At this point, issue the challenge: Take all nine letters and make the mystery word.

Fluency

This poem is easily divided for a small-group Readers Theater performance or for reading aloud with two voices. There are four stanzas, each with four lines. We would suggest that for each stanza, one group or individual read the first two lines and another group or individual read the second two lines. The final stanza can be read in unison. Provide students with ample time to practice before performing for their peers.

Picture Book Pairings

Just a Dream (Van Allsburg, 1990). A boy has a distressing dream of a future world full of pollution.

Uno's Garden (Base, 2006). A beautiful garden and the animals that live there are nearly destroyed by pollution.

"A Worm" by Jack Prelutsky (p. 97)

Found In: *My Dog May Be a Genius* (Prelutsky, 2008)

Summary of Poem: Life is the same for a worm, day after day.

Phonemic Awareness: Initial Consonant—/w/

Read the poem through once, just so children can enjoy the language. Next, as you reread the poem orally, ask children to clap when they hear the /w/ sound. Reread it one more time, but pick up the pace a little, so children hear the repetition of the /w/ sound.

Meaning Vocabulary: Prefixes

Understanding prefixes is a vital component of vocabulary instruction, and this poem contains the words *unaware* and *inaudible*. The prefixes *un-*, and *in-*, along with *re-* and *dis-*, are the four most common, and knowing them will help children figure out the meaning of over 1,500 words (Cunningham, 2009b). To study the prefix *un-*, ask students to reread some familiar material and record any *un-* words on index cards. When they return with their words, guide students as they differentiate between words with the prefix *un-* and words with *un* as the first syllable (such as *under*). Next, help children write a sentence using each *un-* word. Collect the words and sentences for future practice and review.

Meaning Vocabulary to Highlight for ELLs

Prelutsky's poem is filled with challenging vocabulary. To assist ELLs with understanding the meaning of the poem, select three key words and provide student-friendly definitions along with visuals.

> *unaware*: not knowing what is happening
> **Visual:** Read a few pages from *Officer Buckle and Gloria* (Rathmann, 1995) to show that Officer Buckle is unaware of Gloria's actions.

> *solitude*: a state of being away from other people
> **Visual:** Show a picture of a child reading a book alone.

> *emitting*: making or sending out (in this case, a sound)
> **Visual:** Play a tune on your CD player or iPod to demonstrate how it emits a sound.

Picture Book Pairings

Bob and Otto (Bruel, 2007). Otto the worm is shocked to find out that his friend Bob is really a caterpillar.

The Worm Family (Johnston, 2004). The Worm family is undaunted even when faced with prejudice everywhere they try to live.

Frogs and Toads: More Poems and Mini-Lessons

"Polliwogs" by Kristine O'Connell George (p. 1)

Found In: *The Great Frog Race and Other Poems* (George, 1997)

Summary of Poem: Readers share in the excitement of finding a group of polliwogs.

Phonics: Short Vowels—/u/

Introduce or review the short-*u* sound. Provide students with a copy of the poem and a highlighter. Send them on a hunt through the poem for short-*u* words. Once they have found the short-*u* words, add the challenge of thinking of other words that rhyme with the highlighted words.

Fluency

A "rhythm walk" is a motivating activity that pairs movement with fluency instruction (Peebles, 2007). To prepare for a rhythm walk, read the text and decide where the natural breaks occur. Write each chunk of text on a sentence strip. Place strips in order, in a path (straight or curved) around your classroom. Each strip should be one step away from the next. Starting at the first strip, students read the text aloud, take a step to the next phrase, and keep reading. Once they're finished, line students up to start over.

Writing

The goal of this mini-lesson is to highlight Kristine O'Connell George's clever use of exclamation points to make the poem come alive. To begin, read the poem with no expression. Discuss the students' reactions to your reading. Reread the poem again with expression and note the differences. (A picture book that also uses a lot of exclamation points is *Hurry! Hurry!* [Bunting, 2007]). During writing workshop, invite students to look for places in their own writing where an exclamation point might be needed.

Picture Book Pairings

Tadpoles (James, 1999). Molly compares the growth of her tadpoles to her new baby brother's growth.

The Mysterious Tadpole (Kellogg, 2002). Louis's pet tadpole does not turn into an ordinary frog.

"The Pond's Chorus" by Joanna Ryder (p. 9)

Found In: *Toad by the Road: A Year in the Life of These Amazing Amphibians* (Ryder, 2007)

Summary of Poem: In this poem, a chorus of ten toads performs.

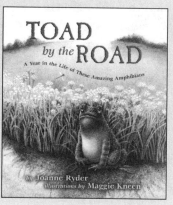

Fluency

This poem is naturally divided into ten parts for Readers Theater, one for each number, 1 to 10.

Sight Vocabulary: Number Word Bingo

The number words one through ten appear in this poem and in many stories that students will read. Take this opportunity to focus on number words by playing a quick game of word bingo. To get ready to play, students draw a tic-tac-toe board on a sheet of paper, and then write a number word in each space. (See the sample below.) As you call out words, students cover the corresponding word with a chip or marker of some kind.

two	seven	eight
five	three	one
nine	four	six

Writing

Writers use ellipses to increase suspense. Notice that Joanna Ryder uses two sets of ellipses at the end of this poem. Ask students to be on the lookout for ellipses in the poems and books they are reading and to try them in their writing.

Picture Book Pairings

Toad (Brown, 1997). A "clammy, sticky, gooey" toad is almost eaten.

Frogs! (Carney, 2009). This is an easy-to-read nonfiction book.

Mini-Lessons for "Fossils Here, Fossils There" by Maria Walther and Katherine Phillips

FLUENCY

Model how some poems can be set to music, singing this poem to the tune of "Old MacDonald Had a Farm." As with other poems throughout the book, groups can continue to practice, polishing rhythm and expression before signing up to present it during a Poetry Break.

COMPREHENSION: BUILDING BACKGROUND KNOWLEDGE

Use this poem, coupled with Aliki's book listed at right, to introduce the concepts of fossils to your young learners. If possible, bring in real fossils for students to examine.

Picture Book Pairings for "Fossils Here, Fossils There"

- -

Fossils Tell of Long Ago (Aliki, 1990)
Learn how fossils are formed and what they tell us about the past.

Mary Anning: Fossil Hunter (Walker, 2001)
The life and accomplishments of the fossil hunter are showcased in this readable biography.

FOSSILS HERE, FOSSILS THERE

by Maria Walther and Katherine Phillips

(Sung to the tune of "Old MacDonald Had a Farm")

Fossils can be made from bones
Of creatures long ago.
They can also be a print
Of plants from long ago.

There are fossils here
and fossils there
Fossils are discovered everywhere!
Fossils can be made from bones
Of creatures long ago!

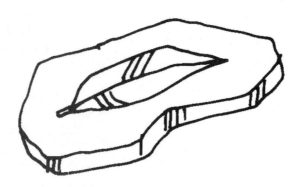

Prehistoric Life: More Poems and Mini-Lessons

"Dinosaur Bone" by Alice Schertle (p. 23)

Found In: *Spectacular Science: A Book of Poems* (Hopkins, 1999)

Summary of Poem: What secrets are hidden inside a dinosaur bone? Ask and you just might find out.

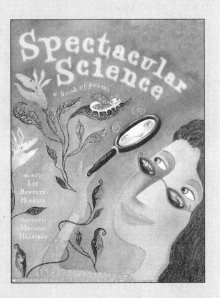

Comprehension: Questioning

In Schertle's poem the narrator asks questions to learn more about the time of the dinosaurs. Skilled readers ask questions as they are reading to clarify understanding of events or facts they are reading. Discuss the fact that if the narrator's questions were answered, he or she would know a lot more about dinosaurs. Model and think aloud in future read-alouds to demonstrate questioning. Invite students to share their questions before, during, and after reading. During guided reading provide students with a sticky note to jot questions as they read.

Sight Vocabulary

Struggling readers may have difficulty recognizing the "question words" *who, what, where, when,* and *why.* Use this poem as a springboard to introduce and practice them. To review the words, students can create a quick game of Sight-Word Memory. To make word cards for the game, provide each student with ten small rectangles of paper. Students write each word on two word cards. Next, working with a partner, they place all 20 word cards face down. Player one chooses two word cards; if the words are the same, he or she gets to keep the match. If not, player one puts them back in the same spot, and it's player two's turn. Play continues until all the matching question words are found.

Options for Differentiation

Provide a visual for each question word and post them in the room for all to see.
> Who? (person)
> What? (a confused face)
> Where? (house)
> When? (clock)
> Why? (question mark)

Picture Book Pairings

I'm Bad (McMullan & McMullan, 2008). A hungry *T. rex* hunts for food without any luck.

Dinosaurs! (Gibbons, 2008). This is an introduction to the five main types of non-bird dinosaurs.

"Sleeping Beside a Stegosaurus on an Overnight Class Trip to the Museum" by Kalli Dakos (p. 16)

Found In: *Put Your Eyes Up Here and Other School Poems* (Dakos, 2003)

Summary of Poem: A child compares him/herself to a dinosaur.

Sight Vocabulary

The sight word *you* is repeated seven times in this poem, making the poem ideal for repeated reading with an emphasis on that word.

Meaning Vocabulary: Antonyms

Teach a review lesson on antonyms. Using the words *big/small, short/tall,* and *wild/tame* from this poem, follow the format for the lesson on page 68.

Writing

Kalli Dakos chose to end her poem with the repeated phrase "Is the same, the same, the same." Repetition is a common poetic element. Ask students to be on the lookout for repetition as they read other poems and poetic picture books. Encourage them to give this technique a try in their own poems.

Picture Book Pairings

Can I Have a Stegosaurus, Mom? Can I? Please!? (Grambling, 1995). A boy begs his mother for a pet dinosaur.

Time Train (Fleischman, 1991). Miss Pym's class takes a train ride through time to study the dinosaurs.

POETIC PICTURE BOOKS AND ANTHOLOGIES FOR SCIENCE	
Title	**Brief Summary**
Arabella Miller's Tiny Caterpillar (Jarret, 2008)	In this rhyming picture book, Arabella finds a tiny caterpillar and watches it grow.
Blast Off! Poems About Space (Hopkins, 1995)	Space enthusiasts will choose this easy-to-read book of poems.
Click, Rumble, Roar: Poems About Machines (Hopkins, 1987)	This anthology consists of poems about machines such as bulldozers, garbage trucks, and helicopters.
Flit, Flutter, Fly! Poems About Bugs and Other Crawly Creatures (Hopkins, 1992)	This collection is an assortment of 20 easy-to-read poems about insects and their brethren.
Fossil (Ewart, 2004)	Ewart presents a lyrical picture book about a girl who finds a fossil.
Lizards, Frogs, and Polliwogs (Florian, 2001)	This playful poetry anthology about reptiles and amphibians is distinguished by delightful word play and memorable illustrations.
Oddhopper Opera: A Bug's Garden of Verses (Cyrus, 2001)	Cyrus explores the fascinating and gross scientific details of the wiggly creatures found on the ground.
Scien-trickery: Riddles in Science (Lewis, 2004)	Children are charmed by this collection of science-related riddles in verse.
Tadpole Rex (Cyrus, 2008)	As a tadpole turns into a frog, he feels just as strong as the huge *Tyrannosaurus rex*.
Toad by the Road: A Year in the Life of These Amazing Amphibians (Ryder, 2007)	Ryder details the life cycle of a toad through engaging poems accompanied by interesting toad facts.

Robust Vocabulary Teaching

Translating Research Into Sensible Daily Practice

While there is abundant research to support the fact that vocabulary development is crucial for students' reading and writing success, researchers also tell us that there is no single best way to teach that vocabulary (Blachowicz & Fisher, 2000; Farstrup & Samuels, 2008). That's actually good news. The key for us to understand is that we need a variety of sound approaches that we can match to the needs of our students (Farstrup & Samuels, 2008; Graves, 2008). A common question is, "What words do I teach?" Again, your decisions are based upon your students. There are times when it is critical to teach three or four words explicitly before a particular lesson, but that will only account for a relatively small number of words a child learns. The majority of words a child knows must be acquired in other ways. Thus, we encourage you to follow the general practices of urging students to read widely, having lively classroom conversations, helping students to learn from firsthand experiences whenever possible, and motivating learners to develop a level of word consciousness that prompts them to collect new words (Blachowicz, Fisher, Ogle, & Watts-Taffe, 2006; Pressley, 2000). In addition, fill your classroom with a rich array of language experiences so that new words are learned and practiced through reading, writing, listening, viewing, and speaking (Blachowicz & Fisher, 2000). You can tell that there is no shortcut to building vocabulary.

MEANING VOCABULARY

Building a word base requires direct teaching and plenty of reading by children themselves. Researcher Isabel Beck and her colleagues offer an effective instructional sequence when teaching meaning vocabulary to young readers (Beck, McKeown, & Kucan, 2002, pp. 65–66):

1. Read the text.
2. Contextualize the word within the text.
3. Have the children say the word.
4. Provide a child-friendly explanation of the word.
5. Provide examples of the word used in contexts different from the story context.
6. Engage children in activities to get them to interact with the words.

When it comes to decisions about which words to teach, these researchers suggest focusing on Tier Two words, those that "are likely to appear frequently in a wide variety of texts and in the written and oral language of mature language users" (Beck et al., 2002, p. 16). Such words come mostly from interactions with books. Children should be able to explain these words using basic, familiar words they already know. Those basic words are Tier One words that don't usually require direct teaching.

SIGHT VOCABULARY

Seeing a word and recognizing it instantly is a necessary ingredient for fluency and comprehension. As a result, it is important to devote quality time to teaching sight words or high-frequency words to our students (Pressley, 2000). Respected scholar Patricia Cunningham (2009a) reminds us that high-frequency words are difficult to learn because most of them have no "concrete consistent" meaning. See the chart below for suggestions on helping young readers strengthen their sight and meaning vocabularies through poetry and beyond.

USING POETRY TO STRENGTHEN STUDENTS' SIGHT AND MEANING VOCABULARY	
Engage in Frequent, Interactive Read-Alouds and Conversations	Make your read-alouds interactive by stopping to discuss words or parts of the poem with listeners. Provide talk time for students to share ideas with one another and build a deeper understanding of the poem.
Teach Sight Vocabulary	Poems are filled with sight words. Capitalize on the teachable moments to identify, chant, and practice sight words. Add the computer for motivating practice. Explore the sight words section of www.literacyconnections.com.
Schedule Ample Time for Independent Reading	Find books and poems at your students' independent reading levels. Provide a place for them to store their "just-right" texts and schedule plenty of time for them to read, read, read.
Provide Real, Hands-On, Concrete Experiences	If there are words in the poem that are new to students: • Gather real objects or images taken with a digital camera. • Bookmark Web sites that have video clips and other resources to build an understanding of the words. • Act out the words yourself. • Play "Word Charades," where students act out the words for one another.
Teach Word Parts: Compound Words, Prefixes, and Suffixes	• To teach compound words, explain that they are single words that contain two complete words. Create a web with a key word in the center circle and other words that would complete the compound word written on the spokes radiating from the center. For example, put *sun* in the center. Then write *light* on one spoke, *shine* on another, *burn* on the third, and so on. For variety, add small illustrations. • Teach the four most common prefixes (*un-*, *re-*, *in-*, and *dis-*) using a similar web activity. Write a prefix on a large classroom chart. Explain the meaning and give students several examples drawn from the poems you are reading. Offer a Prefix Challenge, inviting students to find other words with the sample prefix to be added to the chart. Highlight several additions each day. Use a similar activity with common suffixes such as *-ful*, *-less*, *-able*, and *-ible*.

Demonstrate How to Use Context Clues	When encountering an unfamiliar word in a poem, teach students to "read around the word":
	• Reread the sentences, looking for familiar words to help you figure out the new word.
	• Read the sentence before and after the sentence containing the new word. Look for clues there.
	• If still in doubt, ask a friend or check the dictionary.
Introduce New Words With Child-Friendly Definitions	Select two or three Tier Two words in the poem that might cause confusion. Before reading, explain the words using familiar vocabulary that the children understand. Return to discuss these words after reading the poem and provide multiple exposures to words so that they readily become a part of the children's usable vocabulary.
Create Opportunities for Students to Interact With Words	Create a Word Treasure Hunt to review new words found in poems. Divide students into teams of four early in the day. Give each team the same list of ten words. Invite them to search for them during independent reading or around the school as they walk from place to place, recording where each one is found. When teams turn in their completed lists, note the time on them. Near the end of the day, share results. The winning team might earn more independent reading time.

CHAPTER 7

EXPERIENCE! POEMS FOR THE SEASONS

Experience the Seasons

No matter what the new season is, its arrival seems to excite children. If you live in an area that has distinctive seasons, you are destined to have distracted children as those seasons come and go. The brisk autumn air invites you to take your class on a walk to crunch through fragrant fallen leaves and collect memorable moments for writing. The first snowflakes rivet students' attention on the world outside of the classroom windows. A warm spring day is typically more enticing than your carefully planned lessons. Then, early summer days pull eager children (and teachers) from classrooms and into weeks that promise swimming, camping, playing ball, and savoring leisure time. Capture your distracted learners by celebrating seasonal changes throughout the year with the poetry selections in this chapter, augmented by other favorites you find.

SPRING

Mini-Lessons for "Groundhog" by Maria Fleming

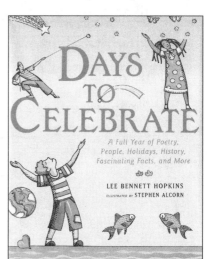

PHONICS: WORD SORT—/-EE/ VS. /-EA/

Contrast the long-*e* sound in the words *treat*, *reasons*, and *seasons* with the long-*e* sound in *flee* and *decree*, all found in the poem. To explore the difference between words with the *-ee* pattern and words contain-

GROUNDHOG
by Maria Fleming

People shoo me
from their lawn,
scold me,
chase me,
want me gone,
treat me like
some kind of pest,
a most unwelcome
garden guest.

Then one day,
for mysterious reasons,
they crown me—

ME!—

King of Seasons.

Will spring come soon?
Will winter flee?
The world awaits
my royal decree.

Source: *Days to Celebrate: A Full Year of Poetry, People, Holidays, History, Fascinating Facts, and More* (Hopkins, 2005)

ing the -ea pattern, students can complete the word sort at right. A reproducible version is provided in the Appendix on page 142. For word sorting tips see page 33.

treat	tweet	heat	greet
sheet	beat	feet	street
seat	fleet	wheat	neat
meet	pleat	sweet	cheat

COMPREHENSION: PREDICTING

Predicting before and during reading is another way to strengthen comprehension. Capitalize on this "predicting" day to slip in a little reading strategy instruction. On February 1, discuss whether children think the groundhog will see his shadow tomorrow. Talk about what kind of weather produces shadows. Then transfer predicting to a read-aloud using the "Stopping to Think" strategy (Taberski, 2000). Write the following questions on a chart. Refer to them as you read and discuss an unfamiliar picture book.

What do you think is going to happen?
Why do you think this is going to happen?
Can you prove it by going back to the text?

First, have readers predict what the book might be about after reading the title and looking at the cover. As you read and students continue to make predictions, prompt them with the questions above. Encourage readers' careful reflection about their predictions. Ask them to explain *why* they made their predictions, and ask them to refer back to the text to prove them. Remind students that predictions are not "right" or "wrong" as long as text backs up their thinking. Note that our predictions don't always match the authors' ideas.

> **Picture Book Pairings for "Groundhog"**
> --------------------
>
> *Groundhog Day!* (Gibbons, 2007)
> Teach your students about groundhogs and the traditions that led to Groundhog Day.
>
> *Substitute Groundhog* (Miller, 2006)
> Groundhog, who has the flu, holds auditions to find a substitute for the big day.

MEANING VOCABULARY: WORD CONCEPT CHART

Work with students in a shared writing format to complete a Word Concept Chart (Cunningham, 2009b) like the one pictured below and on page 146 in the appendix, using the word *pest* from the poem.

Pest

Definition (in own words):	Characteristics:
A person or animal that bothers others	annoying doesn't stop bugging you even when asked
Examples: groundhogs flies my baby brother	**Non-Example:** my best friend

Students can use this chart for other words and concepts throughout the year.

Slipping Into Spring: More Poems and Mini-Lessons

"Galoshes" by Rhoda Bacmeister (p. 18)

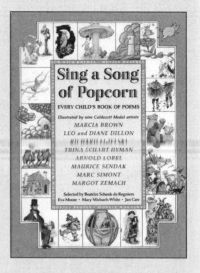

Found In: *Sing a Song of Popcorn: Every Child's Book of Poems* (de Regniers, 1988)

Summary of Poem: Susie puts her galoshes to good use as she walks through all kinds of weather.

Phonics: Blends—/sl/ and /st/

Concentrate on the consonant blends /sl/ and /st/ in this poem found in the words *slooshes, sloshes, slowly, slush, slippery, stamp,* and *stuck.* Follow the lesson suggestion on page 38 for working with blends.

Fluency

After reading this poem aloud to students, invite them to read along chorally, joining in on as many words as they can. Read it together one more time, this time giving the noisy words a little more emphasis. Practice with reading partners, offering each other support, as they prepare to present it during a Poetry Break.

Writing

Work with words that sound like the noise they are describing. Examples are plentiful in this poem, with options like *splishes, sploshes, sloshes,* or *tramp.* Read these words and talk about the images they create. Review other examples of onomatopoeia that you have collected and have displayed on a chart of "Words That Make Noise." Invite students to write two sentences containing onomatopoeia to share with the class. Encourage writers to try some of these words in their own writing.

Picture Book Pairings

Are You Ready to Play Outside? (Willems, 2008). The rain almost stops Elephant and Piggie from playing outside.

Come On, Rain! (Hesse, 1999). A sudden summer rainstorm brings a mother and daughter out to play.

"March Wind" by Anonymous (pp. 26–27)

Found In: *Weather* (Hopkins, 1994)

Summary of Poem: The wind describes its activities as it works and plays throughout the day.

Fluency

After reading the poem to the class, talk together about all of the things the wind does. Read through it again, inviting children to think of other things they have experienced on a windy day. Then, read it chorally. On another day, break the poem into lines. One child at a time can read a line, taking on the voice of the wind.

Comprehension: Point of View

This poem is written in first person from the wind's perspective. Discuss the reasons a poet might choose to do this. Then, students can compare "March Wind" to Pat Hutchins's picture book *The Wind Blew* (1974), which is written in the third person. See page 99 for another poem and picture book pairings for teaching point of view.

Meaning Vocabulary: Action Verbs

Before reading the poem, write several action verbs, such as *jump, run, sing, hop*, on the document camera, overhead, or board. Explain that these verbs show action, telling what someone is doing. Read through the first verse of the poem, asking the children to watch for such verbs. Next, ask for volunteers to come up and underline examples, like *whistle, toss, whirl, strew, blow, shake*, and *sweep*. After enjoying the poem, place children into groups of four or five to play Word Charades with action verbs.

Options for Differentiation

As with the other poems in this book, record these and place the cassette tape or CD in a plastic bag in the listening center with a handy copy of the poem tucked inside. Struggling readers can read along with audio support for enjoyment or for practice.

Picture Book Pairings

The Wind Blew (Hutchins, 1974). In this classic rhyming tale, the wind wreaks havoc.

Whoosh! Went the Wind (Derby, 2006). A boy tries to convince his teacher that the wind made him late for school.

SUMMER

Mini-Lessons for "A Cabin" by Katie Walther

FLUENCY

This poem provides an opportunity to chant together. Give students practice time so they can join in as much as possible. Chanting can give struggling students support as they read what they can and hear the words they are still mastering.

COMPREHENSION: AUTHOR'S PURPOSE

Discuss why the author might have written a poem about a cabin. Ask questions to spur thinking, such as "Do you think the author enjoys being at the cabin?" "What clues does the author give you?" "How does this poem make you feel?" "Would you like to visit this cabin?"

A CABIN
by Katie Walther

North of us is a cabin

A cabin

A cabin

A cabin on a lake

A lake

A lake

A lake which is beautiful

Beautiful

Beautiful

Beautiful trees with birds chirping

Chirping

Chirping

Chirping is heard inside a cabin

Inside a cabin

Inside a cabin

Inside a cabin is a family

A family

A family

A family inside a cabin

A cabin

A cabin

Source: *Impressions of Youth* (The American Library of Poetry, 2004)

WRITING

Invite students to write a poem about a memorable vacation, a family celebration, or a favorite school event. They might like to try this author's repetitive format or use the poem as inspiration to write in their favorite form. Polish and post on a bulletin board highlighting favorite events or memorable places.

Picture Book Pairings for "A Cabin"

The Waterfall's Gift (Ryder, 2001)
This is a beautiful book about a young girl's visit to a waterfall near her grandmother's house.

S Is for S'Mores: A Camping Alphabet (James, 2007)
Readers run through the alphabet, savoring the joys of camping.

Take Me Out to the Ballgame: Poems and Mini-Lessons

"Playing Outfield" by Isabel Joshlin Glaser (p. 3)

Found In: *Extra Innings: Baseball Poems* (Hopkins, 1993)

Summary of Poem: A young baseball player describes a winning game.

Phonics: Words Families— (-op)
Write the words *drop*, *plop*, and *whop* where everyone can see them. Ask readers to take three minutes to jot down other words that end with these two letters to create a helpful -op word family chart. Urge thinkers to try some of the consonant blends you have practiced in the past to make longer words. Add these words to a word sort, having students separate words into two word families, or sort words that are nouns from words that are verbs.

Meaning Vocabulary
Select four words from the poem that you think readers will need to know to understand the poet's message. Examples might include *thunk*, *shivering*, *plastered*, and *flier*. Give child-friendly definitions for these words before reading the poem for the first time. Then, read the poem aloud while learners follow along on their own copies. When done, ask readers to think of a time when sweat "shivered" down their backs or their clothing was "plastered" to their skin. Making personal connections facilitates remembering new vocabulary. For additional practice, use these words in conversation and in the morning message throughout the week.

Writing
The poet uses some creative conventions in this poem, such as ellipses, parentheses, and "big and bold" text. Highlight and discuss each convention and the ways in which it adds to the meaning of the poem. A book to pair with this lesson is *Rollercoaster* by Marla Frazee (2003), in which Frazee uses many of the same conventions. Invite writers to experiment with creative conventions in their own pieces.

Picture Book Pairings
The Bat Boy and His Violin (Curtis, 1998). A young bat boy's violin music inspires the team.

H Is for Home Run: A Baseball Alphabet (Herzog, 2004). The sport receives its due through words and excellent illustrations.

"Baseball Surprise" by Nikki Grimes (Unpaged)

Found In: *Oh, Brother!* (Grimes, 2008)

Summary of Poem: A young boy aspires to be an excellent baseball player now that he has help from his older brother.

Fluency

As your students read this poem, guide them to use the punctuation as markers for pausing and stopping. The periods tell them to stop for a beat, and the commas tell them to pause briefly. Then, model how to read the poem with expression, changing the tone of your voice to highlight specific words.

Phonics: Long Vowels—Silent e

Review the role the silent e plays at the end of a word. Write *home*, *plate*, *change*, and *rate* on a chart for easy viewing. Ask the learners to read the words together as they listen to the vowel sound. Is it long or short? Do they hear one vowel or two? Answers should confirm that the first vowel is long and the last vowel is silent. Work briefly on a list of other silent-e words to add to a special word wall titled "Our Working Words Wall." These are important words that students work with on a daily basis. Using this wall will aid young learners in remembering the role of the silent e as they build skills in word recognition and spelling.

Meaning Vocabulary

Take time to establish understanding about who A-Rod is, what it means to "own" home plate, what it means that his batting doesn't "rate," and what would happen if a ball cleared Saturn's moon. While this clarification will be helpful to all students, it will be especially important to your ELLs.

Picture Book Pairings

Girl Wonder: A Baseball Story in Nine Innings (Hopkinson, 2003). This is a fictional account of Alta Weiss, the first female to pitch for an all-male semi-pro team.

Willie and the All Stars (Cooper, 2008). In 1942 Willie attends an exhibition game between Negro League and Major League all-stars at Wrigley Field.

WINTER

Mini-Lessons for "Snow" by Mary Ann Hoberman

PHONICS: THE DIFFERENT SOUNDS OF /OW/

Make a list of words that have the /ō/ sound, as in the word *snow* from the poem. Read through the words together. Discuss how sometimes when we see the letters *o-w*, especially at the end of a word, they sound like /ō/. Then, write the word *down* for the children to consider. Ask them to read the word together. What do they discover about the letters *o-w*? They can stand for different sounds. Add several other words that have the second sound, such as *town, clown, growl,* and *frown,* next to the other list. Review these words using a word sort.

FLUENCY

After reading and practicing this poem several times, clap out the rhythm. Get students up and moving by walking around the room to the rhythm as the poem is chanted. Change the phrase *snow on the sidewalk* to *rain on a spring day* and enjoy the poem all over again.

MEANING VOCABULARY: COMPOUND WORDS

Review word attack skills when working with compound words using the lesson on page 79. In the poem "Snow," practice with the words *outside, sandbox, sidewalk,* and *everywhere.* Then, puzzle together how to work with *everywhere.* This is an excellent time to emphasize that all compound words are not as concrete and easily "seen" as *sidewalk* and *sandbox.*

> ### Picture Book Pairings for "Snow"
> ----------
>
> *Snowballs* **(Ehlert, 1995)**
> Meet not just one snowman, but a creatively garbed snow family.
>
> *Recess at 20 Below* **(Aillaud, 2005)**
> Join a class as they venture out for recess—in Alaska.

SNOW

by Mary Ann Hoberman

Snow

Snow

Lots of snow

Everywhere we look and everywhere we go

Snow in the sandbox

Snow on the slide

Snow on the bicycle

Left outside

Snow on the steps

And snow on my feet

Snow on the sidewalk

Snow on the sidewalk

Snow on the sidewalk

Down the street.

Source: *The Llama Who Had No Pajama: 100 Favorite Poems* (Hoberman, 1998)

Let It Snow: Snow Poems and Mini-Lessons

"We'll Play in the Snow" by Karla Kuskin (p. 176)

Found In: *Moon, Have You Met My Mother? The Collected Poems of Karla Kuskin* (Kuskin, 2003)

Summary of Poem: There are many opportunities for play when it snows.

Phonics: Differentiating Between Rimes and Rhymes

In this poem you'll find words with the same rimes, or spelling patterns, such as *play*, *stray*, and *stay*, and others that rhyme but have different spelling patterns, like *pies* and *eyes*. Use the lesson on page 37 to contrast these word patterns.

Meaning Vocabulary: Categorizing

Looking at relationships between words or thinking about the kinds of words they use can aid children in remembering new words. After reading and enjoying this poem, write the names of three different categories at the top of a sheet of chart paper. You might choose ACTION VERBS, DESCRIPTIVE WORDS, and THINGS. Go through the poem and write the words under the appropriate category headings. Work though two or three words per category, and then have children work in small groups to complete their lists. Compare and discuss the results to clarify any confusion.

Action Verbs	Descriptive Words	Things
play	snow white	park
stray	dark	snow
clown	fat	snow man

Writing

Children in the poem make snow pies in a big snow pan. Build on that by bringing in several recipe books. Project a recipe on the document camera, overhead, or board. Talk about measurements, ingredients, and directions as you highlight how recipes are written. Tap into prior knowledge by asking what kinds of things children have helped cook at home. Then, write a short recipe poem together about "making a classroom," brainstorming a number of ingredients. Put them into a recipe together. Finally, ask students to study "We'll Play in the Snow" and write a recipe for a snowy day. Edit, polish, and share.

Picture Book Pairings

All You Need for a Snowman (Schertle, 2002). Children work together to build two towering snowmen.

The Snow Show (Fisher, 2008). This clever book opens on the stage of a cooking show, where the hosts demonstrate the steps in making snow.

"Silence" by Eve Merriam (p. 58)

Found In: *The Singing Green* (Merriam, 1992)

Summary of Poem: A quiet snowfall is described.

Phonemic Awareness: Initial, Medial, and Final Sound—/t/

Practice sound isolation with words from this poem. Ask the students to listen for the sound

/t/. Is it at the beginning, middle, or end? Say *quiet*, *float*, and *with-out*. Now, where is it in the word *floating*? Then, practice with the sound /f/, using *floating*, *falling*, and *feathers*. Where do children hear it in *snowflake*?

Fluency

Talk together about how the tone of your voice can make a difference when reading a poem. Students can whisper or recite this in quiet voices as they read it chorally.

Comprehension: Compare and Contrast

Use a Venn diagram to examine the different words the poet uses in this poem as compared to a loud poem like "Shout" on page 62 or "City Music" on page 71. Discuss how the choice of words can convey different ideas and feelings in what we read and write.

Picture Book Pairings

The Three Snow Bears (Brett, 2007). This version of "The Three Bears" reflects the Inuit culture.

The Snowy Day (Keats, 1967). A young child savors a day in the snow by bringing home a souvenir snowball that melts overnight.

FALL

Frolicking Fall Fun: Poems and Mini-Lessons

"Fall Is Here" by Helen H. Moore (p. 58)

Found In: *A Poem a Day* (Moore, 1997)

Summary of Poem: The coming of fall brings many familiar sights and sounds.

Phonemic Awareness: Listening for Rhymes

Tell the students you are going to play a listening game. They are to listen to three words that you say. If all the words rhyme, they are to tap their heads three times. If they do not, they are to shake their heads three times. Try sets of words like these:

>   *fall, tall, small*   *year, ear, gone*   *end, bend, friend*   *red, bed, long*

Return to the words that didn't rhyme and ask students to think of one word to substitute so that they do rhyme.

Comprehension: Extending Meaning

Spend a little more time with this poem by illustrating it using a rebus format. Make a copy of "Fall Is Here" for each student, but leave out lines that would be easily illustrated. Place a copy of the complete poem on the overhead projector or a chart for easy viewing. On their own copies, using colored pencils or crayons, children illustrate the missing lines. Upon completion of the poem, children can work in pairs or triads, reading the poem rebus style, using their illustrations to help them remember the words and referring to the complete poem when they need a bit of support in translating their pictures into the poetic words.

Writing

Read Moore's poem from a writer's perspective. Notice how she uses the repeated phrase "Fall is . . ." to begin many of her lines. Young writers can use this element in their own poetry. Encourage them to pick a topic of interest, such as soccer, a shark, fishing, a dog, and so on. Demonstrate by writing your own poem about a beloved topic (like chocolate)!

> **Chocolate**
> Chocolate is gooey,
> Chocolate is flowing fudge over ice cream,
> Chocolate's something I can't live without
> And
> Chocolate is my friend.

Invite writers to compose their own poem.

Options for Differentiation

Not all children experience fall as described in this poem. Visit Internet sites to investigate fall in different parts of the United States and the world. Use what children discover to write a poem about fall and what it's like for a child who lives somewhere other than your region.

Picture Book Pairings

Leaf Man (Ehlert, 2005). Using leaf collages, Ehlert takes readers on a journey though the countryside with the Leaf Man.

Poppleton in Fall (Rylant, 1999). Rylant uses repetition and rhyme in these three fall stories about Poppleton and his neighbor, Cherry Sue.

"Labor Day" by Marci Ridlon (p. 80)

Found In: *Days to Celebrate: A Full Year of Poetry, People, Holidays, History, Fascinating Facts, and More* (Hopkins, 2005)

Summary of Poem: Why is the first Monday in September a special day? Read this poem to find out.

Phonics: Diphthong—/oi/

Write the word *toil* for easy viewing. Read it aloud and give a child-friendly definition. Circle the letters o-i, and pronounce the sound they represent. Note that the two vowels make their own special sound when they team up. Working with alphabet cards or magnetic letters, ask the students to spell *oil* as you model it. Next, ask them to add the letter *s*. What word do they now have? What does this word mean? They can make *boil*, *broil*, *foil*, *join*, and a challenge word like *noise* or *choice* as you practice this unusual vowel combination.

Sight Vocabulary

Review the days of the week and months of the year with the students. You might chant them together or play a word bingo game with a mixture of the days and months on each playing card.

Meaning Vocabulary to Highlight for ELLs

It is essential that we help our ELLs learn and understand the academic vocabulary that surrounds content area instruction. Use this poem as a starting place to learn and discuss social studies–related words such as *labor* and *workers*. Then, read a book about community helpers, such as *Community Helpers From A to Z* (Kalman, 1998). Invite students to role-play a community helper doing his or her job and see if others can guess that helper's occupation.

Picture Book Pairings:

Labor Day (Schuh, 2003). The history of Labor Day is described with simple text and photos.

Night Shift (Hartland, 2007). While children sleep, there are street sweepers, newspaper printers, and zookeepers awake doing all kinds of interesting things.

POETIC PICTURE BOOKS AND THEMED ANTHOLOGIES	
Title	**Brief Summary**
In November (Rylant, 2000)	A celebrated poet presents an ode to the sights and smells of autumn.
It's Thanksgiving (Prelutsky, 1982)	This collection includes 12 grin-inducing poems about turkey day.
Lemonade Sun and Other Summer Poems (Dotlich, 1998)	Child-friendly poems about the joys of summer are accompanied by bright illustrations.
Rattletrap Car (Root, 2001)	Noisy words abound in this book about a family trip to the beach in an unreliable car.
Red Sled (Thomas, 2008)	Rhyming pairs of words tell the story of a father and son's nighttime sledding adventure.
Snow (Rylant, 2008)	Enjoy Rylant's lyrical picture book's celebration of snow.
Swing Around the Sun (Esbensen, 2003)	An updated edition of Esbensen's seasonal poems is illustrated by four different artists.
To Be Like the Sun (Swanson, 2008)	A child watches a beautiful sunflower grow from a small seed.
The Twelve Days of Springtime: A School Counting Book (Rose, 2009)	A teacher and her class celebrate spring to the tune of "The Twelve Days of Christmas."
Weather (Hopkins, 1994)	This "I Can Read Book" of seasonal poems is divided into five sections: sun; wind and clouds; rain and fog; snow and ice; and weather together.

CHAPTER 8

WRITE! POEMS THAT INSPIRE WRITERS

Surround Budding Writers With Poetry

A basket of poetry books is placed center stage in the classroom library; across the room, near the meeting area, a rhythmic poem about the joys of reading fills the pocket chart. Each student collects treasured poems in a binder so that they are at his or her fingertips during a free moment. Poetic language from picture books is displayed on the walls next to collections of vivid verbs and samples of onomatopoeia. The carefully crafted work of composers is housed on an iPod. On this particular day, the Beatles tune "Good Day Sunshine" is playing as the students greet their teacher, and they leave later

humming the refrain of "Take Me Home, Country Roads" by John Denver. Tongue twisters trip off tongues during word study and jump-rope rhymes ring out at recess. When it comes to writing poetry, the children in this classroom will be ready. Why? Because their teacher has taken a few simple steps to immerse her students in poetry. In this chapter, we've collected poems that will inspire young writers, along with practical tips and ideas for turning your classroom into a place where language play is a part of each and every day.

TEACHING IDEA

In her book *Reading With Meaning*, Debbie Miller (2002) suggests using songs to signal the transition from one activity to the next. This is just one more way to incorporate poetry throughout your busy day. For a suggested list of transition songs created by Katie Walther, see page 149 in the appendix.

PENCILS

by Barbara Esbensen

The rooms in a pencil
are narrow
but elephants   castles and
watermelons
fit in

In a pencil
noisy words yell for attention
and quiet words wait their turn

How did they slip
into such a tight place?
Who
gives them their
lunch?

From a broken pencil
an unbroken poem will come!
There is a long story living
In the shortest pencil

Every word in your
pencil
is fearless   ready to walk
the blue tightrope lines
Ready
To teeter and smile
down   Ready to come right out
and show you
thinking!

Source: *A Jar of Tiny Stars: Poems by NCTE Award-Winning Poets* (Cullinan, 1996)

Mini-Lessons for "Pencils" by Barbara Esbensen

TEACHING IDEA

Use this poem to kick off a genre study of poetry during writing workshop. Begin with a discussion of the "big idea" of Esbensen's poem. Ask learners, "What do you think the poet is trying to tell us as writers?" Listen and record students' thinking on a chart to refer to during future conversations about poetry writing.

MEANING VOCABULARY: QUIET WORDS AND NOISY WORDS

Create a list of quiet words and noisy words for student to use in their own poetry.

Quiet Words	Noisy Words
hush	bang
pitter-patter	crash
rustle	boom
chirp	clang
hiss	smash

WRITING

This mini-lesson is designed to provide writers with a list of possible poetry topics. In the poem "Pencils," the poet shares all the ideas that might be hiding inside a pencil. Discuss what topics and ideas children might have hiding inside their pencils. Demonstrate making a list of the topics you have inside your pencil, and then guide students as they create their own list of topics using the pencil idea sheet found on page 148 in the appendix.

Options for Differentiation

For writers who are struggling to think of topics, take an idea hike around the school grounds. Talk about all the poetry possibilities, such as the broken swing, the window that looks into your classroom, and so on. Remind students to bring their writer's notebooks or a small piece of paper and a pencil to jot down ideas.

Picture Book Pairings for "Pencils"

A Sign (Lyon, 1998)
George Ella Lyon shares how her dreams and experiences helped her to become a writer.

Word Builder (Paul, 2009)
Readers learn that writers build their stories in the same way that construction workers build a city—one step at a time.

A Poem to Pair With "Pencils"

"The Magic Wand" by Kalli Dakos (p. 50)

Found In: *Put Your Eyes Up Here and Other School Poems* (Dakos, 2003)

Summary of Poem: The teacher portrayed in this poem, Ms. Roy, keeps a magic wand on her desk to remind all of her students that they have magic inside of them.

Comprehension: Conversing and Connecting

Talking with our students and facilitating conversations among them builds comprehension. To begin a discussion of this poem, ask the students to find examples in the poem of ways we are all alike. You might underline them on the copy you are all viewing. Then, ask students to give you examples of ways they are special and unlike anyone else, and record them. Extend this group thinking by inviting students to write a few sentences about what makes them unique, referring to the ideas you have generated together and adding others that come to mind.

Options for Differentiation

ELLs might draw a picture that illustrates their uniqueness. If you have access to a digital camera, snap pictures of each student to use as part of their illustrations. Students can then explain and discuss their pictures with a reading buddy. More adept students might write a poem and illustrate it with a photograph from class or from home.

Sight Vocabulary

Write the sight words *the, of, is, and, a, to,* and *it* on large index cards. Ask a volunteer to choose a word card, locate that sight word in the enlarged copy of the poem, and carefully highlight the word by drawing a box around it. Once all seven words have been located, invite children to circle other sight words they know. You'll notice that all seven sight words appear in the first 10 words of the Fry Instant Word list (widely available on the Internet). These words make up about 24 per cent of all written material. That's amazing, isn't it?

the	of	and	a	to
in	is	you	that	it

Remind students that they can review sight words on the word wall or practice them with word cards when they have a little free time.

Writing

To support children as they begin gathering topics for their writing, spend some time in a whole-class brainstorming session to come up with possible ideas. For beginning writers, record the ideas on chart paper to reference throughout the year. Invite more accomplished writers to select six ideas to record on their magic wand idea sheet found in the appendix on page 147. Have students store this in their writing folders for easy access, adding to it whenever a new idea occurs to them.

Options for Differentiation

Meet with students individually or in a small group to continue the discussion about where they can get ideas for their writing. Ask them about activities they like to do, favorite sports, pets, or family events to trigger ideas. Help them select five personally appealing ideas to keep in their writing folders, meeting with them again in upcoming weeks to support writing efforts and add to the list.

Picture Book Pairings

Ms. McCaw Learns to Draw (Zemach, 2008). Just like Ms. Roy, Ms. McCaw is able to see the magic inside of her students, in this case, Dudley, a struggling learner.

Miss Malarkey Leaves No Reader Behind (Finchler & O'Malley, 2006). Miss Malarkey vows to find a book for even the most reluctant reader.

Mini-Lessons for "Quiddling With Words" by Kristine O'Connell George

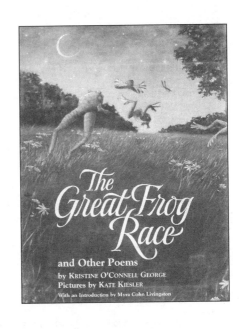

PHONICS: CONSONANT BLENDS—/BR/, /CR/, /GR/

Print the words in the poem that contain beginning -r blends (*brittle, cracker,* and *grasshopper*) on a piece of chart paper with three columns labeled with "br-," "cr-," and "gr-." Explain to the children that sometimes when two letters work together at the beginning of a word, and we clearly hear each letter in the pair, they belong in a special family called "blends." Model stretching the sounds of the blends from this poem so that children can hear how they work. Ask students to talk to a partner and come up with a few more blends for each list. Add them to the chart and post for easy reference. Stop here and reread the poem. Challenge the students to find the word that has a three-letter *r*-blend at the beginning (*spring*). Conclude the mini-lesson by rereading the poem once again and inviting students to clap when they hear a word with one of these blends.

COMPREHENSION: VISUALIZING

When students can visualize or make mental images when they read, they are facilitating comprehension. In this poem, the poet uses such descriptive words that students can readily sketch what the verse tells them.

QUIDDLING WITH WORDS

by Kristine O'Connell George

I like words

like *Perforate*

that snap neatly

into brittle pieces

like a cracker,

like *Ricochet*

that spring madly

like a grasshopper

in a glass pickle jar,

like *Quiddle*

which I just discovered

in the dictionary

sandwiched between

Perforate and *Ricochet*.

Source: *The Great Frog Race and Other Poems* (George, 1997)

Ask students to visualize as you snap several crackers into pieces, highlighting the words *brittle* and *snap*. Then, ask students to sketch what they think the word *perforate* might look like if it were snapped into brittle pieces. Finally, let them try drawing their images of *ricochet* and *quiddle*, sharing the results with a classmate.

Options for Differentiation

An engaging option to the mini-lesson above is teaching students how to create a word sketch. Once modeled, this activity could be used as a guided reading or literacy center activity. Provide students with a copy of the Vocabulary Sketch Card found in Appendix 3 on page 145. Students choose a word from the poem and locate the definition in the dictionary. Then, they draw an illustration on the card that includes the word of choice and represents that definition. Another option is to draw the word in such a way that the letters themselves define it. For example, if the word is *fire*, students should draw the letters as if they are on fire. Thus, the word depicts the definition. Set aside time for students to share their sketches with the class. Then post them on a bulletin board alongside the poem.

MEANING VOCABULARY: DICTIONARY USAGE

Teach dictionary usage and reinforce how it serves as a student's reading helper. For this lesson, look up the words together as a class. Demonstrate the process using the word *perforate*. If a definition is confusing, be sure students have a student-friendly definition handy.

A student-friendly dictionary recommended by well-known vocabulary expert Isabel Beck and her colleagues is *Collins COBUILD Dictionary* (Sinclair et al., 1987). In this helpful resource, words are defined in an easy-to-understand manner. Other words from the poem to look up and learn their meanings include *brittle*, *ricochet*, and *quiddle*.

Picture Book Pairings for "Quiddling With Words"

The Boy Who Loved Words (Schotter, 2006)
Selig is a collector of words who discovers his purpose is to share these words with others.

Max's Words (Banks, 2006)
Max collects, sorts, and organizes his word collection to create thoughts and stories.

A Poem to Pair With "Quiddling With Words"

"Treasure Words" by Rebecca Kai Dotlich (p. 88)

Found In: *Days to Celebrate: A Full Year of Poetry, People, Holidays, History, Fascinating Facts, and More* (Hopkins, 2005)

Summary of Poem: This poem celebrates the beauty and magic of words.

Teaching Idea

Words *are* magic. We can use them in so many different ways. Sometimes our struggling students get so bogged down trying to decode while reading or to spell while writing, they lose the joy of the written word. Use this poem as a reminder to all of the power of words.

Phonemic Awareness: Initial Consonant—/s/

Read the poem through once, just so children can enjoy the language. Next, as you reread the poem orally, ask children to listen for words with the initial /s/ sound. On the third reading, invite students to quickly draw an s shape in the air each time they hear the /s/ sound. Finally, to help students differentiate between /s/ and other consonant sounds, say two words and ask students to repeat the word with the initial /s/ sound.

Writing

Dotlich's poem is filled with description that makes words sound so enticing. Enlarge the poem and place it where children can easily see it. Start the activity by asking children to look for words that describe all the things words can be. Ask them to volunteer to come up to circle a descriptive word. As a word is circled, ask the class what else is "quiet," "loud," and so forth. After seven or eight words have been identified, discuss how such descriptive words can be used in their own writing. Add them to a writing word wall or to a chart titled "Writing Words" for future use.

Picture Book Pairings

The Word Wizard (Falwell, 1998). While eating her alphabet cereal, Anna discovers the joy of playing with words.

Posy (Newbery, 2008). Show students how a writer cleverly uses words to describe a kitten's busy day.

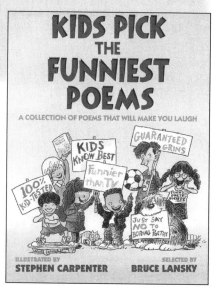

Mini-Lessons for "Clatter" by Joyce Armor

PHONICS: WORD FAMILIES—(-ACK) AND (-OCK)

Focus on two of the high-utility word families with which children need to be familiar, *-ack* (*quack*) and *-ock* (*ticktock*). Write the two

CLATTER
by Joyce Armor

If I should list my favorite words,
They'd sound a lot like this:
Rumble, crash, snort, jangle, thump,
Roar, fizzle, splat, moo, hiss.
Not to mention gobble, clang,
Tweet, sputter, ticktock, growl;
Crackle, chirp, boom, whistle, wheeze,
Squawk, jingle, quack, thud, howl.
Then of course there's grunt, toot, cuckoo,
Thunder, bang, pop, mush,
Rattle, splash, rip, ding-dong, and . . .
My parents' favorite—*Hush!*

Source: *Kids Pick the Funniest Poems* (Lansky, 1991)

rimes at the top of a sheet of chart paper. Read each rime aloud with the students echoing them after you. Then, as you add an onset to each rime, ask your learners to chant the two parts before blending them together. It would sound like this: *qu + -ack = quack, t + -ock = tock.* Reread the words you've created. Point out how readers chunk the endings as they decode other words in the same word families. Put students to work in small groups to come up with more words to add to each word-family list. Record accurate suggestions under the appropriate word family, chorally reread the words, and then post the completed lists for future reference.

FLUENCY

After reading this poem a number of times, consider an active Readers Theater performance. For example, an enjoyable way to perform this poem would be to assign each child an example of onomatopoeia from the poem to say in a distinctive way—for example, reading *ding-dong* like a bell or *quack* as a duck might make the sound. Then, reading from a displayed copy of the poem, each child will chime in when it is his or her turn.

WRITING

Get the students out of the classroom to go on an Environmental Word Expedition. Gather several classroom helpers, divide students into small groups led by an adult, and head down the hallway through the school. Armed with paper and pencil, children are to listen for sounds they can turn into words. Move out to the playground where the thunk of a ball, the smack of a ball and bat, or the screech of the chain on the swing will provide them with words for writing. Return to the classroom and compile all of the finds. Fill a chart with these onomatopoeic words to serve as fuel for future writing assignments.

> ### Picture Book Pairings for "Clatter"
> ----------
>
> *Achoo! Bang! Crash! The Noisy Alphabet* (MacDonald, 2003)
> This alphabet book is filled with onomatopoeic words.
>
> *Snow Sounds: An Onomatopoeic Story* (Johnson, 2006)
> This unique, nearly wordless picture book is peppered with descriptive words that accent the visual narrative.

A Poem to Pair With "Clatter"

"Whirr, Whirr, Zing, Zap" by Betsy Franco (pp. 20–21)

Found In: *Messing Around on the Monkey Bars and Other School Poems for Two Voices* (Franco, 2009)

Summary of Poem: The sounds of a classroom come alive in this poem written for two voices.

Fluency

Franco's book contains poems designed for two voices. To strengthen fluency, begin by chorally reading the poem. Then, divide students into two groups or into poetry pairs. Provide ample time for them to practice, with your encouragement and coaching. Have them perform for one another or another class, or make a surprise trip to the school office to perform for the principal or office staff.

Meaning Vocabulary to Highlight for ELLs

To illuminate the concept of onomatopoeia, write a collection of easy-to-illustrate words on index cards, such as *chirp, whistle,* and *ticktock*. Work with students to create visual images that represent each word by snapping photos with a digital camera or downloading images from the computer. With a classmate or classroom helper, learners work together to use these words in sentences. Have them try the sentences both orally and in writing for future review.

Writing

The subject of Franco's onomatopoeic poem is a busy classroom (including the lawnmower roaring by outside!). As you reread the poem, notice and discuss the pattern she uses. Invite young poets to pick a different setting for a sound-filled poem—the zoo, perhaps, where each animal they meet makes a unique sound, or their kitchen, unusually noisy when dad is making dinner. Model drafting your own poem; then support students as they pen theirs. Once polished, perform poems in two voices.

Picture Book Pairing

If You Were Onomatopoeia (Shaskan, 2008). Vibrant illustrations and playful layouts provide a lively introduction to and numerous examples of words that imitate sounds.

POETS USE SHAPES: ANTHOLOGIES OF SHAPE POEMS	
Title	**Brief Summary**
Come to My Party and Other Shape Poems (Roemer, 2004)	Divided into sections by season, Roemer's anthology includes colorful concrete poems about familiar topics such as bugs, the beach, snow, and more.
Outside the Lines (Burg, 2002)	Concrete poems celebrate playtime activities.
A Poke in the I (Janeczko, 2001)	Well-known visual poets provide a tour of 30 concrete poems.
Splish, Splash (Graham, 1994)	Young poets will enjoy this delightful collection of water-related shape poems—perfect for a science unit on the water cycle.

Teaching Idea

Gather books that contain concrete poems, such as the ones listed in the chart above. In a concrete poem, the poet writes the words in such a way that they form the shape of the object described. For the youngest writers, it is helpful if you select poems about familiar topics to read aloud as mentor poems. You will need a few days to demonstrate how a shape poem is created. As you demonstrate each step, invite learners to do the same in their writer's notebook.

- Choose a topic for your concrete poem. Brainstorm a list of words or phrases to describe the topic.
- Play with words to create a poem of that topic.
- Reread, revise, edit, and polish the poem.
- Draw a pencil outline of the shape of the object. Write the words along the edge of the pencil line. One snag that children encounter is having too many or too few words to match their outline. Possible solutions to this dilemma include repeating a line or adding details to the shape to fit extra words.
- Erase the pencil line. Trace the words with colored pencils or fine-tip markers.
- Share and post for others to enjoy.

(Adapted from Walther & Phillips, 2009)

INSPIRING PICTURE BOOKS AND WRITING IDEAS	
Title	**Writing Ideas**

A Isn't for Fox: An Isn't Alphabet (Ulmer, 2008)	Ulmer's inventive alphabet book is enjoyable to read aloud. Each letter features a playful verse such as,
	
	    A isn't for box;
	    it isn't for fox.
	    A is for ants that
	    crawl over your socks.
	
	Work in a shared writing format to create your own playful "Isn't Alphabet." This may inspire some writers to try a few verses on their own.

Buttercup's Lovely Day (Beck, 2008)	These poems are written from a cow's point of view. After discussing how poets write poems from different perspectives, invite students to write a poem from a viewpoint other than their own.
Crazy Like a Fox: A Simile Story (Leedy, 2008)	Inspire your writers to write their own simile poem or story after reading this one about Rufus the fox. For another book brimming with similes, read *My Dog Is as Smelly as Dirty Socks* (Piven, 2007).

APPENDIX 1: Word Sorts

HARD C, SOFT C WORD SORT CARDS FOR LESSON ON PAGE 33

car	corn	cylinder
caterpillar	city	cub
camp	centipede	cereal
cent	cow	circle
cup	cookie	cycle

fowl	growl	down
clown	town	gown
crown	howl	prowl
jowl	brown	scowl

Teaching Struggling Readers With Poetry © 2010 by Maria Walther and Carol Fuhler, Scholastic Professional.

threw	tow	slow	knew
flew	snow	show	grow
glow	few	blew	chew
brew	new	low	know

meet	seat	sheet	treat
pleat	fleet	beat	tweet
sweet	wheat	feet	heat
cheat	neat	street	greet

Teaching Struggling Readers With Poetry © 2010 by Maria Walther and Carol Fuhler, Scholastic Professional.

APPENDIX 2: Making Words

LETTERS FOR MAKING WORDS LESSON FOUND ON PAGE 71

t	s	p
r	a	i

LETTERS FOR MAKING WORDS LESSON FOUND ON PAGE 78

u	a	s	e
r	e	r	t

Teaching Struggling Readers With Poetry © 2010 by Maria Walther and Carol Fuhler, Scholastic Professional.

l	u	i
o	p	n
o	t	l

Teaching Struggling Readers With Poetry © 2010 by Maria Walther and Carol Fuhler, Scholastic Professional.

APPENDIX 3: Vocabulary Sketch Card

Name: _____

My word: _____

Dictionary definition:

My Picture Definition

APPENDIX 4: Word Concept Chart

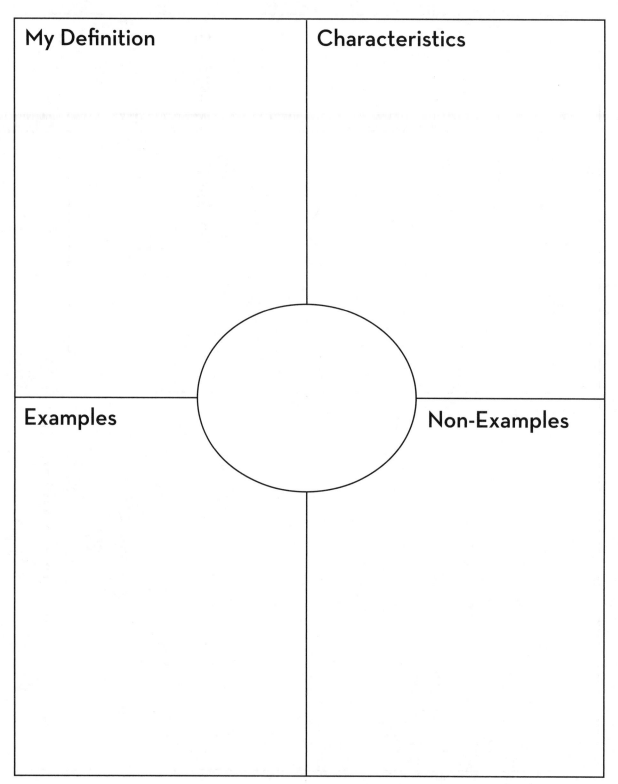

My Definition	Characteristics
Examples	Non-Examples

APPENDIX 5: Idea Sheets

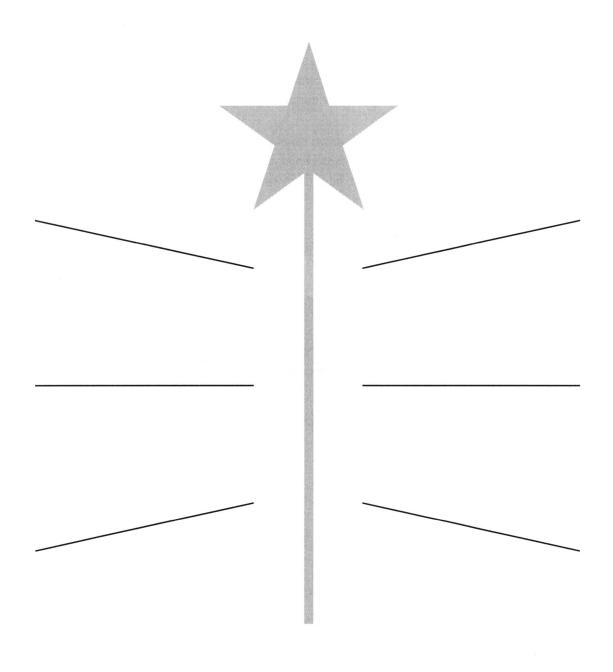

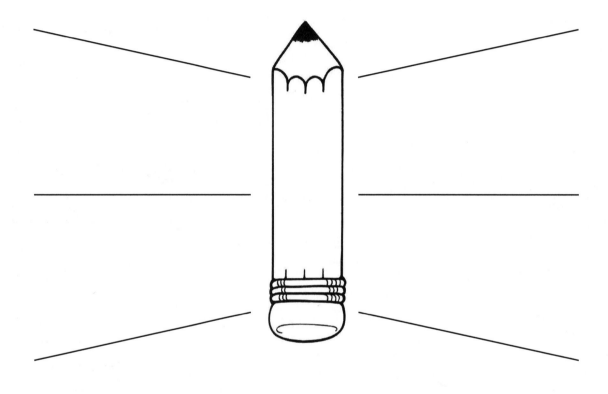

APPENDIX 6: Transition Song List

SONG TITLE	ARTIST	ALBUM
Morning Songs		
Oh, What a Beautiful Morning	Gordon MacRae	*Oklahoma!*
The Morning Report	Various Artists	*The Lion King*
Reading Workshop Songs		
ABC	Jackson 5	*ABC*
Y.M.C.A.	The Village People	*Cruisin'*
Writing Workshop Songs		
Say	John Mayer	*The Bucket List*
Oh, the Thinks You Can Think	Various Artists	*Seussical*
Math Songs		
25 or 6 to 4	Chicago	*Chicago Story: The Complete Greatest Hits*
1234	Feist	*The Reminder*
Lunch Songs		
Food, Glorious Food	Various Artists	*Oliver!*
Green Eggs and Ham	Various Artists	*Seussical*
Recess Songs		
Fun in the Sun	Steve Harwell	*The Princess Diaries 2: Royal Engagement*
Monkey Around	Various Artists	*Seussical*
Music Songs		
Do Re Mi	Various Artists	*The Sound of Music*
Play My Music	Jonas Brothers	*Camp Rock*
Art Songs		
Joseph's Coat	Various Artists	*Joseph and the Amazing Technicolor Dreamcoat*
Colors of the Wind	Various Artists	*Pocahontas*
P. E. Songs		
Get'cha Head in the Game	Various Artists	*High School Musical*
We Are the Champions	Queen	*News of the World*
Going Home Songs		
Take Me Home, Country Roads	John Denver	*Take Me Home, Country Roads*
We're Off to See the Wizard	Various Artists	*The Wizard of Oz*
So Long, Farewell	Various Artists	*The Sound of Music*

Teaching Struggling Readers With Poetry © 2010 by Maria Walther and Carol Fuhler, Scholastic Professional.

PROFESSIONAL RESOURCES CITED

Adams, M. J. (1990). *Beginning to read: Thinking and learning about print.* Cambridge, MA: MIT Press.

Allen, J. (2003). But they still can't (or won't) read! Helping children overcome roadblocks to reading. *Language Arts, 80*(4), 268–274.

Allington, R. L. (2002). What I've learned about effective reading instruction. *Phi Delta Kappan, 83*(10), 740–747.

Allington, R. L. (2005). Proven programs, profits, and practice: Ten unprofitable but scientific strategies for improving reading achievement. In B. Altwerger (Ed.), *Reading for profit: How the bottom line leaves kids behind* (pp. 216–230). Portsmouth, NH: Heinemann.

Allington, R. L. (2006). *What really matters for struggling readers: Designing research-based programs* (2nd ed.). New York: Allyn & Bacon.

Allington, R. L. (2009). *What really matters in fluency: Research-based practices across the curriculum.* New York: Allyn & Bacon.

Anderson, R. C., Hiebert, E. H., Scott, J. A., & Wilkinson, I. A. G. (1985). *Becoming a nation of readers: The report of the commission on reading.* Washington, DC: National Institute of Education.

Bear, D., Invernizzi, M., Templeton, S., & Johnson, F. (2007). *Words their way: Word study for phonics, vocabulary, and spelling instruction* (4th ed.). New York: Allyn & Bacon.

Beck, I., McKeown, M., & Kucan, C. (2008). *Creating robust vocabulary: Frequently asked questions & extended examples.* New York: Guilford.

Beck, I. J., McKeown, M. G., & Kucan, L. (2002). *Bringing words to life: Robust vocabulary instruction.* New York: Guilford.

Beck, I., & McKeown, M. (1996). Conditions of vocabulary instruction. In R. Barr, M. L. Kamil, P. B. Mosenthal, & P. D. Pearson (Eds.). *Handbook of reading research, Vol. II* (pp. 879–814). Mahwah, NJ: Lawrence Erlbaum.

Blachowicz, C. L. Z., & Fisher, P. (2000). Vocabulary instruction. In M. L. Kamil, P. B. Mosenthal, P. D. Pearson, & R. Barr (Eds.), *Handbook of reading research, Vol. III* (pp. 503–523). Mahwah, NJ: Lawrence Erlbaum.

Blachowicz, C. L. Z., Fisher, P. J. L., Ogle, D., & Watts-Taffe, S. (2006). Vocabulary: Questions from the classroom. *Reading Research Quarterly, 41*(4), 524–539.

Braunger, J., & Lewis, J. P. (2006). *Building a knowledge base in reading* (2nd ed.). Newark, NJ: International Reading Association.

Brophy, J., & Good, T. (1986). Teacher behavior and student achievement. In M. Wittrock (Ed.), *The handbook of research on teaching* (3rd ed.). Riverside, NJ: Macmillan.

Cole, A. D. (2003). *Knee to knee, eye to eye: Circling in on comprehension.* Portsmouth, NH: Heinemann.

Cunningham, P. M. (2009a). *Phonics they use: Words for reading and writing* (5th ed.). New York: Allyn & Bacon.

Cunningham, P. M. (2009b). *What really matters in vocabulary: Research-based practices across the curriculum.* New York: Allyn & Bacon.

Cunningham, P. M., & Allington, R. L. (2007). *Classrooms that work* (4th ed.). New York: Allyn & Bacon.

Cunningham, P. M., & Cunningham, J. W. (1992). Making words: Enhancing the invented spelling-decoding connection. *The Reading Teacher, 46*(2), 106–115.

Duke, N. K., & Pearson, P. D. (2002). Effective practices for developing reading comprehension. In S. J. Samuels & A. Farstrup (Eds.), *What research has to say about reading instruction* (3rd ed.) (pp. 145–199). Newark, DE: International Reading Association.

Dunston, P. J. (2002). Instructional components for promoting thoughtful literacy. In C. C. Block, L. B. Gambrell, & M. Pressley (Eds.), *Improving comprehension instruction: Rethinking research, theory, and classroom practice* (pp. 135–151). San Francisco, CA: Jossey Bass.

Farstrup, A. E., & Samuels, S. J. (Eds.). (2008). *What research has to say about vocabulary instruction.* Newark, DE: International Reading Association.

Faver, S. (2008). Repeated reading of poetry can enhance reading fluency. *The Reading Teacher, 62*(4), 350–352.

Fountas, I. C., & Pinnell, G. S. (1996). *Guided reading: Good first reading for all children.* Portsmouth, NH: Heinemann.

Fry, E. B. (1998). Teaching reading: The most common phonograms. *The Reading Teacher, 51*(7), 620–622.

Fuhler, C. J., & Walther, M. P. (2007). *Literature is back! Using the best books for teaching readers and writers across genres.* New York: Scholastic.

Galda, L., & Cullinan, B. E. (2006). *Literature and the child* (6th ed.). Belmont, CA: Wadsworth.

Gambrell, L. B. (2001). What we know about motivation to read. In R. F. Flippo (Ed.), *Reading researchers in search of common ground* (pp. 129–143). Newark, DE: International Reading Association.

Garan, E. M., & DeVoogd, G. (2008). The benefits of sustained silent reading: Scientific research and common sense converge. *The Reading Teacher, 62*(4), 336–344.

Gentry, J. R. (2004). *The science of spelling: The explicit specifics that make great readers and writers (and spellers!).* Portsmouth, NH: Heinemann.

Graves, M. F. (2006). *The vocabulary book: Learning and instruction.* New York: Teachers College Press.

Graves, M. F. (2008). One size does not fit all. In A. E. Farstrup & S. J. Samuels (Eds.), *What research has to say about vocabulary instruction* (pp. 56–79). Newark, DE: International Reading Association.

Graves, M. F., Juel, C., & Graves, B. B. (2007). *Teaching reading in the 21st century.* Boston: Pearson/ Allyn & Bacon.

Gusman, J. (2005). *Practical strategies for accelerating the literacy skills and content learning of your ESL students.* Sacramento, CA: New Horizons in Education.

Hadaway, N. L., Vardell, S. M., & Young, T. A. (2001). Scaffolding oral language development through poetry for students learning English. *The Reading Teacher, 54*(8), 796–806.

Hudson, R., Lane, H., & Pullen, P. (2005). Reading fluency assessment and instruction: What, why, and how? *The Reading Teacher, 58*(8), 702–714.

Johnston, P. (2004). *Choice words: How our language affects children's learning.* Portland, ME: Stenhouse.

Katz, B. (2007). *Partner poems for building fluency: 25 original poems with research-based lessons that help students improve their fluency and comprehension.* New York: Scholastic.

McGill-Franzen, A., Allington, R. L., Yokoi, L., & Brooks, G. (1999). Putting books in the room seems necessary but not sufficient. *Journal of Educational Research, 93*, 67–74.

Miller, D. (2002). *Reading with meaning.* Portland, ME: Stenhouse.

Ming, K., & Dukes, C. (2008). Fluency: A necessary ingredient in comprehensive reading instruction in inclusive classrooms. *TEACHING Exceptional Children Plus, 4*(4), 2–14.

Moore, H. H. (1997). *A poem a day: 180 thematic poems and activities that teach and delight all year long; grades K–3.* New York: Scholastic.

National Education Association. (2000). Report of the NEA Task Force on Reading 2000. Washington, DC. Retrieved April 17, 2009, from http://www.nea.org/ home/18301.htm.

National Reading Panel. (2000). *Teaching children to read: An evidence-based assessment of scientific research literature on reading and its implications for reading instruction: Reports of the subgroups.* Washington, DC: National Institute of Child Health and Human Development. NIH Publication No. 00–4754.

National Research Council (NRC). (1996). *National science education standards.* Washington, DC: National Academy Press.

Oczkus, L., Baura, G., Murray, K., & Berry, K. (2006). Using the love of "poetry" to improve primary students' writing. *The Reading Teacher, 59*(5), 475–479.

Pearson, P. D., & Fielding, L. (1996). Comprehension instruction. In R. Barr, M. L. Kamill, P. B. Mosenthal, & P. D. Pearson (Eds.), *Handbook of reading research, Vol. II* (pp. 815–860). Mahwah, NJ: Lawrence Erlbaum.

Pearson, P. D., Roehler, L. R., Dole, J. A., & Duffy, G. G. (1992). Developing expertise in reading comprehension. In S. J. Samuels & A. Farstrup (Eds.), *What research has to say about reading instruction* (pp. 145–199). Newark, DE: International Reading Association.

Peebles, J. L. (2007). Incorporating movement with fluency instruction: A motivation for struggling readers. *The Reading Teacher, 60*(6), 578–581.

Pinnell, G. S., & Fountas, I. C. (1998). *Word matters: Teaching phonics and spelling in a reading/writing classroom.* Portsmouth, NH: Heinemann.

Pressley, M. (2000). What should comprehension instruction be the instruction of? In M. L. Kamil., P. B. Mosenthal, P. D. Pearson, & R. Barr (Eds.), *Handbook of reading research, Vol. III.* (pp. 545–561). Mahwah, NJ: Lawrence Erlbaum.

Pressley, M. (2002). Improving comprehension instruction: A path for the future. In C. C. Block, L. B. Gambrell, & M. Pressley (Eds.), *Improving comprehension instruction: Rethinking research, theory, and classroom practice* (pp. 385–399). San Francisco, CA: Jossey Bass.

Pressley, M., Dolezal, S. E., Raphael, L., Mohan, L., Bogner, K., & Roehrig, A. (2003). *Motivating primary grade students.* New York: Guilford.

Rasinski, T. V. (2003). *The fluent reader: Oral reading strategies for building word recognition, fluency, and comprehension.* New York: Scholastic.

Rasinski, T. V. (2006). Fluency: An oft-neglected goal of the reading program. In C. Cummins (Ed.), *Understanding and implementing Reading First initiatives* (pp. 60–71). Newark, DE: International Reading Association.

Rasinski, T. V., & Padak, N. D. (2001). *From phonics to fluency: Effective teaching of decoding on reading fluency in elementary school.* New York: Longman.

Rasinski, T. V., & Padak, N. (2004). *Effective reading strategies: Teaching children who find reading difficult* (3rd ed.). Upper Saddle River, NJ: Pearson.

Rasinski, T., Rupley, W. H., & Nichols, W. D. (2008). Two essential ingredients: Phonics and fluency getting to know each other. *The Reading Teacher, 62*(3), 257–260.

Reutzel, D. R., & Cooter, R. B., Jr. (2008). *Teaching children to read: The teacher makes the difference* (5th ed.). Upper Saddle River, NJ: Pearson.

Scanlon, D. M., & Vellutino, F. R. (1997). A comparison of the instructional backgrounds and cognitive profiles of poor, average, and good readers who were initially identified as at risk for reading failure. *Scientific Studies of Reading, 1,* 191–216.

Sekeres, D. C., & Gregg, M. (2007). Poetry in third grade: Getting started. *The Reading Teacher, 60*(5), 466–475.

Sinclair, J., et al. (Eds). (1987). *Collins COBUILD dictionary: English language.* London: Collins.

Stahl, K. A. D. (2004). Proof, practice and promise: Comprehension strategy instruction in the primary grades. *The Reading Teacher, 57*(7), 598–609.

Stanovich, K. E. (1986). Matthew effects in reading: Some consequences of individual differences in the acquisition of literacy. *Reading Research Quarterly, 21*(4), 360–406.

Taberski, S. (2000). *On solid ground.* Portsmouth, NH: Heinemann.

Templeton, S., & Morris, D. (1999). Questions teachers ask about spelling. *Reading Research Quarterly, 34*(1), 102–112.

Tomlinson, C. A. (1999). *The differentiated classroom: Responding to the needs of all learners.* Alexandria, VA: ASCD.

Trelease, J. (2006). *The read-aloud handbook* (6th ed.). New York: Penguin.

Valencia, S. W., & Buly, M. R. (2004). Behind test scores: What struggling readers *really* need. *The Reading Teacher, 57*(6), 520–531.

Vardell, S. M. (2009). Everyday poetry. *Book Links, 18*(3), 44–47.

Walther, M. P., & Phillips, K. A. (2009). *Month-by-month trait-based writing instruction.* New York: Scholastic.

Wicklund, L. K. (1989). Shared poetry: A whole language experience adapted for remedial readers. *The Reading Teacher, 47*(2), 478–481.

Wilfong, L. G. (2008). Building fluency, word-recognition ability, and confidence in struggling readers: The Poetry Academy. *The Reading Teacher, 62*(1), 4–13.

Wood, K. D. (2002). Differentiating reading and writing lessons to promote content learning. In C. C. Block, L. B. Gambrell, & M. Pressley (Eds.), *Improving comprehension instruction: Rethinking research, theory, and classroom practice* (pp. 155–180). San Francisco, CA: Jossey Bass.

Yopp, H. K. (1992). Developing phonemic awareness in young children. *The Reading Teacher, 45*(9), 696–703.

Yopp, H. K, & Yopp, R. H. (2000). Supporting phonemic awareness development in the classroom. *The Reading Teacher, 54*(2), 130–143.

Yopp, H. K., & Yopp, R. H. (2003). Time with text. *The Reading Teacher, 57*(3), 284–287.

CHILDREN'S LITERATURE CITED

Note to readers: If a book is cited in more than one chapter, it is referenced in the first chapter where it appears followed by a list of the additional chapters.

CHAPTER 1: Using Poetry to Teach Struggling Readers

Esbensen, B. J. (2003). *Swing around the sun.* (C. Chee, J. L. Porter, M. GrandPré, & S. Gammell, Illus.). Minneapolis, MN: Carolrhoda. (Ch. 7)

Florian, D. (2001). *Lizards, frogs, and polliwogs.* San Diego, CA: Harcourt. (Ch. 6)

Florian, D. (2007). *Comets, stars, the moon, and Mars: Space poems and paintings.* Orlando, FL: Harcourt.

Florian, D. (2009). *Dinothesaurus.* New York: Beach Lane. (Ch. 3)

Franco, B. (2008). *Bees, snails, & peacock tails.* (S. Jenkins, Illus.). New York: Margaret K. McElderry. (Ch. 3)

Hopkins, L. B. (Ed.). (1999). *Sports! Sports! Sports! A poetry collection.* (B. Floca, Illus.). San Diego, CA: Harcourt.

Maddox, M. (2008). *A crossing of zebras: Animal packs in poetry.* (P. Huber, Illus.). Honesdale, PA: Boyds Mills. (Ch. 3)

Merriam, E. (1992). *The singing green: New and selected poems for all seasons.* (K. C. Howell, Illus.). New York: Morrow. (Ch. 7)

Prelutsky, J. (Ed.). (1983). *The Random House book of poetry for children.* (A. Lobel, Illus.). New York: Random House. (Chs. 2 & 3)

Prelutsky, J. (1996). *A pizza the size of the sun.* (J. Stevenson, Illus.). New York: Greenwillow.

Ruddell, D. (2009). *A whiff of pine, a hint of skunk: A forest of poems.* (J. Rankin, Illus.). New York: Margaret K. McElderry. (Ch. 3)

Shields, C. D. (1997). *Saturday night at the dinosaur stomp.* (S. Nash, Illus.). Cambridge, MA: Candlewick.

Sidman, J. (2006). *Butterfly eye and other poems of the meadow.* (B. Krommes, Illus.). Boston: Houghton Mifflin. (Ch. 4)

Worth, V. (2007). *Animal poems.* (S. Jenkins, Illus.). New York: Farrar, Straus.

CHAPTER 2: Welcome! Poems About School, Friendship, and Family

Adoff, A. (1973). *Black is brown is tan.* (E. A. McCully, Illus.). New York: HarperCollins.

Amato, M. (2008). *The chicken of the family.* (D. Durand, Illus.). New York: Putnam.

Bagert, B. (2007). *Shout! Little poems that roar.* (S. Yoshikawa, Illus.). New York: Dial. (Ch. 4)

Browne, A. (2007). *My brother.* New York: Farrar, Straus.

Carlson, N. (2002). *There's a big, beautiful world out there!* New York: Viking.

Diggory Shields, C. (2003). *Almost late to school: And other school poems.* (P. Meisel, Illus.). New York: Dutton.

Friend, C. (2007). *The perfect nest.* (J. Manders, Illus.). Cambridge, MA: Candlewick.

Greenfield, E. (1991). *Night on Neighborhood Street.* (J. S. Gilchrist, Illus.). New York: Dial.

Grimes, N. (2005). *Danitra Brown, class clown.* (E. B. Lewis, Illus.). New York: HarperCollins.

Grimes, N. (2008). *Oh, brother!* (M. Benny, Illus.). New York: Greenwillow. (Ch. 7)

Harrison, D. L. (2009). *Vacation: We're going to the ocean.* (R. Shepperson, Illus.). Honesdale, PA: Wordsong.

Heard, G. (2009). *Falling down the page: A book of list poems.* New York: Roaring Book Press.

Hopkins, L. B. (Ed.). (1986). *Best friends.* (J. Watts, Illus.). New York: HarperCollins.

Hopkins, L. B. (Ed.). (1990). *Good books, good times.* (H. Stevenson, Illus.). New York: HarperCollins.

Hopkins, L. B. (Ed.). (1996). *School supplies.* (R. Flower, Illus.). New York: Simon & Schuster. (Ch. 5)

Hopkins, L. B. (Ed.). (2004). *Wonderful words: Poems about reading, writing, speaking, and listening.* (K. Barbour, Illus.). New York: Simon & Schuster.

Hopkins, L. B. (Ed.). (2005). *Days to celebrate: A full year of poetry, people, holidays, history, fascinating facts, and more.* (S. Alcorn, Illus.). New York: Greenwillow. (Chs. 4, 7, & 8)

Katz, K. (2002). *The colors of us.* New York: Henry Holt.

Kellogg, S. (1986). *Best friends.* New York: Dial.

Lies, B. (2008). *Bats at the library.* Boston: Houghton Mifflin.

Nikola-Lisa, W. (1994). *Bein' with you this way.* (M. Bryant, Illus.). New York: Lee & Low.

O'Neill, A. (2002). *The recess queen.* (L. Huliska-Beith, Illus.). New York: Scholastic.

Otoshi, K. (2008). *One.* San Rafael, CA: KO Kids Books.

Parr, T. (2003). *The family book.* New York: Little, Brown.

Paschen, E. (2005). *Poetry speaks to children.* Naperville, IL: Sourcebooks.

Prelutsky, J. (1984). *The new kid on the block.* (J. Stevenson, Illus.). New York: Greenwillow.

Prelutsky, J. (2008*). My dog may be a genius.* (J. Stevenson, Illus.). New York: Greenwillow. (Ch. 6)

Sierra, J. (2008). *Born to read.* (M. Brown, Illus.). New York: Knopf.

Steptoe, M. (1997). *In daddy's arms, I am tall.* New York: Lee & Low.

Viorst, J. (1995). *Alexander, who's not (do you hear me? I mean it!) going to move.* (R. Preiss-Glasser, Illus.). New York: Atheneum.

Waber, B. (1988). *Ira says goodbye.* Boston: Houghton Mifflin.

Watt, M. (2008). *Scaredy squirrel.* Toronto: Kids Can.

Ziefert, H. (2001). *39 uses for a friend.* (R. Doughty, Illus.). New York: Putnam.

CHAPTER 3: Adventure! Animal Poems

Andreae, G. (1996). *Rumble in the jungle.* (D. Wojtowycz, Illus.). New York: Scholastic.

Andreae, G. (1998). *Commotion in the ocean.* (D. Wojtowycz, Illus.). New York: Scholastic.

Andreae, G. (2001). *Giraffes can't dance.* (G. Parker-Rees, Illus.). New York: Orchard.

Andreae, G. (2005). *Dinosaurs galore!* (D. Wojtowycz, Illus.). New York: Scholastic.

Arnold, T. (2006). *Hi! Fly Guy.* New York: Cartwheel.

Arnosky, J. (2003). *All about sharks.* New York: Scholastic.

Ata, T., & Moroney, L. (Adapted by). (2003). *Baby rattlesnake/Viborita de cascabel.* (M. Reisberg, Illus.). San Francisco, CA: Children's Book Press.

Bunting, E. (2003). *Whales passing.* (L. Davis, Illus.). New York: Blue Sky.

Carle, E. (1989). *Eric Carle's animals, animals.* New York: Philomel.

Davis, M. S. (2008). *A garden of whales.* (J. B. O'Connell, Illus.). Buffalo, NY: Firefly.

Dodd, E. (2008). *What pet to get?* New York: Arthur A. Levine.

Donaldson, J. (2003). *The snail and the whale.* (A. Scheffler, Illus.). New York: Dial.

Florian, D. (2000). *Mammalabilia.* San Diego, CA: Harcourt.

Hoberman, M. A. (1998). *The llama who had no pajama: 100 favorite poems.* (B. Frazer, Illus.). San Diego, CA: Harcourt. (Ch. 7)

Johnston, T. (2000). *Desert song.* (E. Young, Illus.). San Francisco, CA: Sierra Club.

Kellogg, S. (1971). *Can I keep him?* New York: Dial.

Kuskin, K. (2003). *Moon, have you met my mother? The collected poems of Karla Kuskin.* (S. Ruzzier, Illus.). New York: HarperCollins. (Chs. 5 & 7)

MacLachlan, P., & Charest, E. M. (2006). *Once I ate a pie.* (K. Schneider, Illus.). New York: HarperCollins.

Marsh, T. J. (1999). *Way out in the desert.* Flagstaff, AZ: Rising Moon.

McDermott, G. (1994). *Coyote: A trickster tale from the American Southwest.* San Diego, CA: Harcourt.

Moore, L. (2006). *Beware, take care: Fun and spooky poems by Lillian Moore.* (H. Fine, Illus.). New York: Henry Holt.

Paul, A. W. (2008). *I count on culebra: Go from 1 to 10 in Spanish.* (E. Long, Illus.). New York: Holiday House.

Pearson, S. (2004). *Squeal and squawk: Barnyard talk.* (D. Slonim, Illus.). New York: Marshall Cavendish.

Pearson, S. (2005). *Who swallowed Harold?* (D. Slonim, Illus.). New York: Marshall Cavendish.

Pinkney, A. D. (2006). *Peggony-Po: A whale of a tale.* (B. Pinkney, Illus.). New York: Hyperion.

Prelutsky, J. (1983). *Zoo doings: Animal poems.* (P. O. Zelinsky, Illus.). New York: Greenwillow.

Ruddell, D. (2007). *Today at the bluebird café: A branch-ful of birds.* (J. Rankin, Illus.). New York: Margaret K. McElderry.

Schreiber, A. (2008). *Sharks!* Washington, DC: National Geographic.

Sendak, M. (1988). *Where the wild things are.* New York: HarperCollins.

Spinelli, E. (2007). *Polar bear, Arctic hare.* (E. Fernandes, Illus.). Honesdale, PA: Wordsong.

Taylor, S. (2007). *When a monster was born.* (N. Sharrat, Illus.). New Milford, CT: Roaring Brook.

Urbanovic, J. (2009). *Duck and cover.* New York: HarperCollins.

Ward, J. (2006). *There was a coyote who swallowed a flea.* Flagstaff, AZ: Rising Moon.

Ward, N. (2002). *Don't eat the teacher!* New York: Scholastic.

Wright-Frierson, V. (1996). *A desert scrapbook: Dawn to dusk in the Sonoran Desert.* New York: Simon & Schuster.

CHAPTER 4: Perform! Playing With Poems

Adoff, A. (1995). *Street music: City poems.* (K. Barbour, Illus.). New York: HarperCollins.

Bagert, B. (2007). *Shout! Little poems that roar.* (S. Yoshikawa, Illus.). New York: Dial.

Bagert, B. (1992). *Let me be the boss: Poems for kids to perform.* Honesdale, PA: Boyds Mills.

Bunting, E. (1994). *A day's work.* (R. Himler, Illus.). New York: Clarion.

Burleigh, R. (2009). *Clang! Clang! Beep! Beep! Listen to the city.* (B. Giacobbe, Illus.). New York: Simon & Schuster.

Causley, C., Charles, F., Geisel, T., Hubbell, P., Hymes, J. L., Jr., Ipcar, D., et al. (1997). *Poems go clang: A collection of noisy verse.* (D. Gliori, Illus.). Cambridge, MA: Candlewick.

Cazet, D. (2007). *Will you read to me?* New York: Atheneum.

Fleming, D. (2007). *Beetle bop.* San Diego, CA: Harcourt.

Fox, M. (1997). *Whoever you are.* (L. Straub, Illus.). San Diego, CA: Harcourt.

Franco, B. (2009). *Messing around on the monkey bars and other school poems for two voices.* (J. Hartland, Illus.). Cambridge, MA: Candlewick. (Ch. 8)

Graham, I. (2006). *Trucks and earthmovers.* Chicago: Raintree.

Harter, D. (2000). *The animal boogie.* Cambridge, MA: Barefoot Books.

Hoberman, M. A. (2007). *You read to me, I'll read to you: Very short scary tales to read together.* (M. Emberley, Illus.). Boston: Little, Brown.

Hopkins, L. B. (Ed.). (1987). *Click, rumble, roar: Poems about machines.* (A. H. Audette, Photographer). New York: HarperCollins.

Hopkins, L. B. (2009). *City I love.* (M. Hall, Illus.). New York: Abrams.

Hutchins, P. (1993). *The wind blew.* New York: Aladdin.

Katz, B. (2009). *More pocket poems.* (D. Zemke, Illus.). New York: Dutton.

Lewis, K. (2002). *My truck is stuck!* (D. Kirk, Illus.). New York: Hyperion.

Meister, C. (2000). *Busy, busy city street.* (S. Guarnaccia, Illus.). New York: Viking.

Minters, F. (1994). *Cinder-Elly.* New York: Viking.

Moore, L. (2006). *Beware, take care: Fun and spooky poems by Lilian Moore.* (H. Fine, Illus.). New York: Henry Holt.

Pearson, D. (2006). *Big city song.* (L. R. Reed, Illus.). New York: Holiday House.

Pitcher, C. (2008). *The littlest owl.* (T. Macnaughton, Illus.). Intercourse, PA: Good Books.

Prelutsky, J. (Ed.). (1986). *Read-aloud rhymes for the very young.* (M. Brown, Illus.). New York: Knopf. (Ch. 5)

Recorvits, H. (2003). *My name is Yoon.* (G. Swiatkowska, Illus.). New York: Frances Foster.

Schertle, A. (2008). *The little blue truck.* (J. McElmurry, Illus.). San Diego, CA: Harcourt.

Shapiro, A. L. (1997). *Mice squeak, we speak.* (T. dePaola, Illus.). New York: Putnam.

Sidman, J. (2005). *Song of the water boatman.* (B. Prange, Illus.). Boston: Houghton Mifflin.

Sidman, J. (2006). *Butterfly eyes and other secrets of the meadow.* (B. Krommes, Illus.). New York: Houghton Mifflin.

Tarpley, N. A. (1998). *I love my hair!* (E. B. Lewis, Illus.). Boston: Little, Brown.

Tyler, M. (2005). *The skin you live in.* (D. L. Csicsko, Illus.). Chicago: Chicago Children's Museum.

Walker, A. (2006). *There is a flower at the tip of my nose smelling me.* (S. Vitale, Illus.). New York: HarperCollins.

Warhola, J. (2007). *If you're happy and you know it: Jungle edition.* New York: Orchard.

Yolen, J., & Peters, A. F. (2007). *Here's a little poem: A very first book of poetry.* Cambridge, MA: Candlewick. (Ch. 5)

CHAPTER 5: Imagine! Poems to Take You Away

Anderson, S. (2008). *Islands.* Minneapolis, MN: Lerner.

Anderson, S. (2008). *Mountains.* Minneapolis, MN: Lerner.

Bunting, E. (2009). *My special day at Third Street School.* (S. Bloom, Illus.). Honesdale, PA: Boyds Mills.

Bush, L., & Bush, J. (2008). *Read all about it!* (D. Brunkus, Illus.). New York: HarperCollins.

Carlson, N. (2008). *Henry's amazing imagination!* New York: Viking.

Coy, J. (2000). *Vroomaloom zoom.* (J. Cepeda, Illus.). New York: Crown.

Garland, M. (2003). *Miss Smith's incredible storybook.* New York: Dutton.

Hopkins, L. B. (Ed.). (1995). *Blast off! Poems about space.* (M. Sweet, Illus.). New York: HarperCollins. (Ch. 6)

Hopkins, L. B. (Ed.). (1996). *School supplies: A book of poems.* (R. Flower, Illus.). New York: Aladdin.

Keller, L. (2008). *The scrambled states of America talent show.* New York: Henry Holt.

Laden, N. (1994). *The night I followed the dog.* San Francisco, CA: Chronicle.

Larios, J. (2006). *Yellow elephant: A bright bestiary.* (J. Paschkis, Illus.). San Diego, CA: Harcourt.

LaRochelle, D. (2004). *The best pet of all.* (H. Wakiyama, Illus.). New York: Dutton.

Lehman, B. (2008). *Trainstop.* Boston: Houghton Mifflin.

Martin, B., & Archambault, J. (1986). *Barn dance.* (T. Rand, Illus.). New York: Holt.

McClintock, B. (2008). *Adèle & Simon in America.* New York: Farrar, Straus.

McNulty, F. (2005). *If you decide to go to the moon.* (S. Kellogg, Illus.). New York: Scholastic.

Mitton, T. (2000). *Roaring rockets: Amazing machines.* (A. Parker, Illus.). New York: Scholastic.

Prelutsky, J. (2006). *Behold the bold umbrellaphant: And other poems.* (C. Berger, Illus.). New York: Greenwillow.

Redmond, E. S. (2009). *Felicity Floo visits the zoo.* Cambridge, MA: Candlewick.

Reibstein, M. (2008). *Wabi Sabi.* (E. Young, Illus.). Boston: Little, Brown.

Robertson, M. P. (2001). *The egg.* New York: Dial.

Sierra, J. (2004). *Wild about books.* (M. Brown, Illus.). New York: Knopf.

Simon, S. (2004). *Seymour Simon's book of trains.* New York: HarperCollins.

Stainton, S. (2007). *The chocolate cat.* (A. Mortimer, Illus.). New York: HarperCollins.

Weatherby, M. A. (1997). *My dinosaur.* New York: Scholastic.

Weisner, D. (2006). *Flotsam.* New York: Clarion.

CHAPTER 6: Investigate! Poems to Enhance Science Instruction

Aliki. (1990). *Fossils tell of long ago.* New York: Crowell.

Arnold, C. (2007). *Wiggle and waggle.* (M. Peterson, Illus.). Watertown, MA: Charlesbridge.

Base, G. (2006). *Uno's garden.* New York: Abrams.

Black, I. M. (2009). *Chicken cheeks.* (K. Hawkes, Illus.). New York: Simon & Schuster.

Brown, M. W. (1999). *I like bugs.* (G. B. Karas, Illus.). New York: Random House.

Brown, R. (1997). *Toad.* New York: Dutton.

Bruel, R. O. (2007). *Bob and Otto.* (N. Bruel, Illus.). New Milford, CT: Roaring Book.

Bunting, E. (2007). *Hurry! Hurry!* (J. Mack, Illus.). Orlando, FL: Harcourt.

Carney, E. (2009). *Frogs!* Washington, DC: National Geographic.

Chappelow, S. (2006). *Caterpillars.* Chicago, IL: Raintree.

Cronin, D. (2003). *Diary of a worm.* (H. Bliss, Illus.). New York: Joanna Cotler.

Cyrus, K. (2001). *Oddhopper opera: A bug's garden of verses.* San Diego, CA: Harcourt.

Cyrus, K. (2008). *Tadpole Rex.* Orlando, FL: Harcourt.

Dakos, K. (2003). *Put your eyes up here and other school poems.* (G. Brian Karas, Illus.). New York: Simon & Schuster. (Ch. 8)

Ewart, C. (2004). *Fossil.* New York: Walker.

Fleischman, P. (1991). *Time train.* (C. Ewart, Illus.). New York: HarperCollins.

Florian, D. (2001). *Lizards, frogs, and polliwogs.* San Diego, CA: Harcourt.

George, K. O. (1997). *The great frog race and other poems.* (K. Kiesel, Illus.). New York: Clarion. (Ch. 8)

Gibbons, G. (2008). *Dinosaurs!* New York: Holiday House.

Grambling, L. G. (1995). *Can I have a stegosaurus, Mom? Can I? Please!?* (H. B. Lewis, Illus.). Mahwah, NJ: BridgeWater.

Hoose, P., & Hoose, H. (1998). *Hey, little ant.* (D. Tilley, Illus.). Berkeley, CA: Tricycle.

Hopkins, L. B. (Ed.). (1992). *Flit, flutter, fly!: Poems about bugs and other crawly creatures.* (P. Palagonia, Illus.). New York: Doubleday.

Hopkins, L. B. (Ed.). (1999). *Spectacular science: A book of poems.* (V. Halstead, Illus.). New York: Simon & Schuster.

James, B. (1999). *Tadpoles.* New York: Dutton.

Jarrett, C. (2008). *Arabella Miller's tiny caterpillar.* Cambridge, MA: Candlewick.

Jenkins, S., & Page, R. (2003). *What do you do with a tail like this?* Boston: Houghton Mifflin.

Jenkins, S., & Page, R. (2006). *Move!* Boston: Houghton Mifflin.

Johnston, T. (2004). *The Worm family.* (S. Innerst, Illus.). Orlando, FL: Harcourt.

Kellogg, S. (2002). *The mysterious tadpole.* New York: Dial.

Lansky, B. (Ed.). (2004). *Rolling in the aisles: A collection of laugh-out-loud poems.* (S. Carpenter, Illus.). New York: Meadowbrook. (Ch. 6)

Lewis, J. P. (2004). *Scien-trickery: Riddles in science.* (F. Remkiewicz, Illus.). Orlando, FL: Silver Whistle.

Madison, A. (2007). *Velma Gratch & the way cool butterfly.* (K. Hawkes, Illus.). New York: Schwartz & Wade.

Martin, B., Jr. (2009). *The Bill Martin Jr. big book of poetry.* New York: Simon & Schuster.

McDonald, M. (1995). *Insects are my life.* (P. B. Johnson, Illus.). New York: Orchard.

McMullan, K., & McMullan, J. (2008). *I'm bad.* New York: Joanna Cotler.

Pedersen, J. (2008). *Houdini the amazing caterpillar.* New York: Clarion.

Rathmann, P. (1995). *Officer Buckle and Gloria.* New York: Putnam.

Rockwell, A. (2002). *Becoming butterflies.* (M. Halsey, Illus.). New York: Walker & Company.

Ryder, J. (1989). *Where butterflies grow.* (L. Cherry, Illus.). New York: Lodestar.

Ryder, J. (2007). *Toad by the road: A year in the life of these amazing amphibians.* (M. Kneen, Illus.). New York: Henry Holt.

Van Allsburg, C. (1990). *Just a dream.* Boston: Houghton Mifflin.

Vicker, L. (2006). *Poetry parade.* Ames, IA: Unpublished personal teaching materials.

Walker, S. (2001). *Mary Anning: Fossil hunter.* (P. V. Saroff, Illus.). Minneapolis, MN: Carolrhoda.

Worth, V. (1994). *All the small poems and fourteen more.* (N. Babbitt, Illus.). New York: Farrar, Straus,

CHAPTER 7: Experience! Poems for the Seasons

Aillaud, C. L. (2005). *Recess at 20 below.* Portland, OR: Graphic Arts Center Publishing Company.

The American Library of Poetry. (2004). *Impressions of youth.* Houlton, ME: Author.

Brett, J. (2007). *The three snow bears.* New York: Putnam.

Cooper, F. (2008). *Willie and the all-stars.* New York: Philomel.

Curtis, G. (1998). *The bat boy and his violin.* (E. B. Lewis, Illus.). New York: Simon & Schuster.

de Regniers, B. S. (1988). *Sing a song of popcorn: Every child's book of poems.* New York: Scholastic.

Derby, S. (2006). *Whoosh! Went the wind.* (V. Nguyen, Illus.). New York: Marshall Cavendish.

Dotlich, R. K. (1998). *Lemonade sun and other summer poems.* (J. S. Gilchrist, Illus.). Honesdale, PA: Boyds Mills.

Ehlert, L. (2005). *Leaf Man.* San Diego, CA: Harcourt.

Ehlert, L. (2005). *Snowballs.* San Diego, CA: Harcourt.

Fisher, C. (2008). *The snow show.* Orlando, FL: Harcourt.

Frazee, M. (2003). *Rollercoaster.* Orlando, FL: Harcourt.

Gibbons, G. (2007). *Groundhog Day!* New York: Holiday House.

Hartland, J. (2007). *Night shift.* New York: Bloomsbury.

Herzog, B. (2004). *H is for home run: A baseball alphabet.* Chelsea, MI: Sleeping Bear.

Hesse, K. (1999). *Come on, rain!* (J. Muth, Illus.). New York: Scholastic.

Hopkins, L. B. (Ed.). (1993). *Extra innings: Baseball poems.* (S. Medlock, Illus.). San Diego, CA: Harcourt.

Hopkins, L. B. (Ed.). (1994). *Weather.* (M. Hall, Illus.). New York: HarperCollins.

Hopkinson, D. (2003). *Girl wonder: A baseball story in nine innings.* New York: Atheneum

Hutchins, P. (1974). *The wind blew.* New York: Macmillan.

James, H. F. (2007). *S is for s'mores: A camping alphabet.* (L. Judge, Illus.). Chelsea, MI: Sleeping Bear.

Kalman, B. (1998). *Community helpers from A to Z.* New York: Crabtree.

Keats, E. J. (1962). *The snowy day.* New York: Viking.

Miller, P. (2006). *Substitute groundhog.* (K. Ember, Illus.). New York: A. Whitman.

Moore, H. H. (1997). *A poem a day.* New York: Scholastic.

Prelutsky, J. (1982). *It's Thanksgiving.* (M. Hafner, Illus.). New York: Greenwillow.

Root, P. (2001). *Rattletrap car.* (J. Barton, Illus.). Cambridge, MA: Candlewick.

Rose, D. L. (2009). *The twelve days of springtime: A school counting book.* (C. Armstrong-Ellis, Illus.). New York: Abrams.

Ryder, J. (2001). *The waterfall's gift.* (R. J. Watson, Illus.). San Francisco, CA: Sierra Club.

Rylant, C. (1999). *Poppleton in fall.* (M. Teague, Illus.). New York: Blue Sky.

Rylant, C. (2000). *In November.* (J. Kastner, Illus.). San Diego, CA: Harcourt.

Rylant, C. (2008). *Snow.* (L. Stringer, Illus.). Orlando, FL: Harcourt.

Schertle, A. (2002). *All you need for a snowman.* (B. Lavallee, Illus.). New York: Silver Whistle.

Schuh, M. C. (2003). *Labor Day.* Mankato, MN: Pebble.

Swanson, S. M. (2008). *To be like the sun.* Orlando, FL: Harcourt.

Thomas, P. (2008). *Red sled.* (C. L. Demarest, Illus.). Honesdale, PA: Boyds Mills.

Willems, M. (2008). *Are you ready to play outside?* New York: Hyperion.

CHAPTER 8: Write! Poems That Inspire Writers

Banks, K. (2006). *Max's words.* (B. Kulikov, Illus.). New York: Farrar, Straus.

Beck, C. (2008). *Buttercup's lovely day.* (A. Beck, Illus.). Custer, WA: Orca.

Burg, B. (2002). *Outside the lines.* (R. Gibbon, Illus.). New York: G. P. Putnam's Sons.

Cullinan, B. (Ed.). (1996). *A jar of tiny stars: Poems by NCTE award-winning poets.* Honesdale, PA: Boyds Mills.

Falwell, C. (1998). *The word wizard.* New York: Clarion.

Finchler, J., & O'Malley, K. (2006). *Miss Malarkey leaves no reader behind.* (K. O'Malley, Illus.). New York: Walker.

Graham, J. B. (1994). *Splish, splash.* (S. Scott, Illus.). New York: Ticknor & Fields.

Janeczko, P. B. (Ed.). (2001). *A poke in the I.* (C. Raschka, Illus.). New York: Scholastic.

Johnson, D. A. (2006). *Snow sounds: An onomatopoeic story.* Boston: Houghton Mifflin.

Lansky, B. (Ed.). (1991). *Kids pick the funniest poems.* (S. Carpenter, Illus.). New York: Simon & Schuster.

Leedy, L. (2008). *Crazy like a fox: A simile story.* New York: Holiday House.

Lyon, G. E. (1998). *A sign.* (C. Soentpiet, Illus.). New York: Orchard Books.

MacDonald, R. (2003). *Achoo! Bang! Crash! The noisy alphabet.* New York: Roaring Brook.

Newbery, L. (2008). *Posy.* (C. Rayner, Illus.). New York: Atheneum.

Paul, A. W. (2009). *Word builder.* (K. Cyrus, Illus.). New York: Simon & Schuster.

Piven, H. (2007). *My dog is as smelly as dirty socks and other funny family portraits.* New York: Schwartz & Wade.

Roemer, H. B. (2004). *Come to my party and other shape poems.* (H. Takahashi, Illus.). New York: Henry Holt.

Schotter, R. (2006). *The boy who loved words.* (G. Potter, Illus.). New York: Schwartz & Wade.

Shaskan, T. S. (2008). *If you were onomatopoeia.* (S. Gray, Illus.). Minneapolis, MN: Picture Window.

Ulmer, W. (2008). *A isn't for fox: An isn't alphabet* (L. Knorr, Illus.). Chelsea, MI: Sleeping Bear.

Zemach, K. (2008). *Ms. McCaw learns to draw.* New York: Arthur A. Levine.